FROM Grace TO Embrace

Inspirational True Stories
of God's Faithfulness

JUDY JULIEN

Waterlily
PRESS

From Grace to Embrace: Inspirational True Stories of God's Faithfulness

© 2020 by Judy Julien

All rights reserved. No part of this publication may be reproduced, distributed, or transmitted in any form or by any means, including photocopying, recording, or other electronic or mechanical methods, without the prior written permission of the publisher, except in the case of brief quotations embodied in critical reviews and certain other noncommercial uses permitted by copyright law.

Printed in the United States of America

Published in Bloomington, Illinois by Waterlily Press.

Designed by Jennifer Ghionzoli

Author photograph by Judy Julien, using iPhone.

Unless otherwise indicated, Scripture quotations taken from the Holy Bible, *New International Version*,® *NIV*,® Copyright © 1973, 1978, 1984, 2011 by Biblica, Inc.®. Used by permission. All rights reserved worldwide.

Scripture quotations marked KJV taken from the *Holy Bible* King James Version. Public domain.

Scripture quotations marked CEB taken from the Common English Bible®, CEB.® Copyright © 2010, 2011 by Common English Bible.™ Used by permission. All rights reserved worldwide.

Scripture quotations marked NLT are taken from the *Holy Bible*, New Living Translation, copyright © 1996, 2004, 2015 by Tyndale House Foundation. Used by permission of Tyndale House Publishers, Carol Stream, Illinois 60188. All rights reserved.

Scripture quotations marked ESV are from the ESV® Bible (The Holy Bible, English Standard Version®), copyright © 2001 by Crossway, a publishing ministry of Good News Publishers. Used by permission. All rights reserved.

Scripture quotations marked NASB taken from the New American Standard Bible® (NASB), Copyright © 1960, 1962, 1963, 1968, 1971, 1972, 1973, 1975, 1977, 1995 by The Lockman Foundation. Used by permission. www.Lockman.org

Scripture quotations marked GNT are from the Good News Translation in Today's English Version-Second Edition, copyright © 1992 by American Bible Society. Used by permission.

Scripture quotations marked NKJV are taken from the New King James Version,® copyright © 1982 by Thomas Nelson, Inc. Used by permission. All rights reserved.

ISBN: 978-1-7347423-0-5 (HC)
ISBN: 978-1-7347423-1-2 (SC)
ISBN: 978-7347423-2-9 (ebook)

Subjects: Religious-Devotional literature.

LCCN: 2020920217

Table of Contents

Dedication vii
Preface ix
Introduction xi

1. From Grace to Embrace 1
2. I Believe in Miracles 5
3. Silver Lining 9
4. The Blue Ridge Mountains 13
5. Jaws 17
6. A Father's Prayer 21
7. Masterpiece 25
8. Christmas Is a Time for Giving 29
9. The Comfort of Cardinals 33
10. The Wedding 37
11. Grandmother's Porch Swing 41
12. Bucket List Terror 45
13. A Heart of Gold 49
14. Adoption 53
15. Dinner at Grandma's 57
16. Home Alone 61
17. Spread Your Wings 65
18. Zombies 69
19. A Cup of Tea 73
20. Worry Warrior 77
21. The Last Journey Home: Grief 81
22. The Uninvited House Guest 85
23. Fixer Upper 89
24. Christmas at the White House 93
25. Epiphany in the Garden 97
26. He Knows My Name 101
27. God's Angels 105
28. Rekindle the Flame 109
29. Trust Like Noah, Not Jonah 113
30. Forgive and Forget 117
31. The Escape 121
32. Mirror, Mirror 125
33. The Joy of Little Boys 129
34. Be Still 133
35. A New Day 137
36. The Storms Will Come 141
37. I Hereby Banish You Forever 145
38. It's Never Too Late 149
39. God Is Writing Your Story 153
40. Our Days Are Numbered 157

The Gospel 161
Author's Note 163
Acknowledgments 165

Dedication

I dedicate *From Grace to Embrace* to my late mother,
Carol Jean Lott, whose servant heart and love for Christ inspired me
to write these stories. Her influence can be seen on many pages of
this book, as God's reflection from her is seen through me.

Thank you, Mom! Your legacy lives on,
Judy

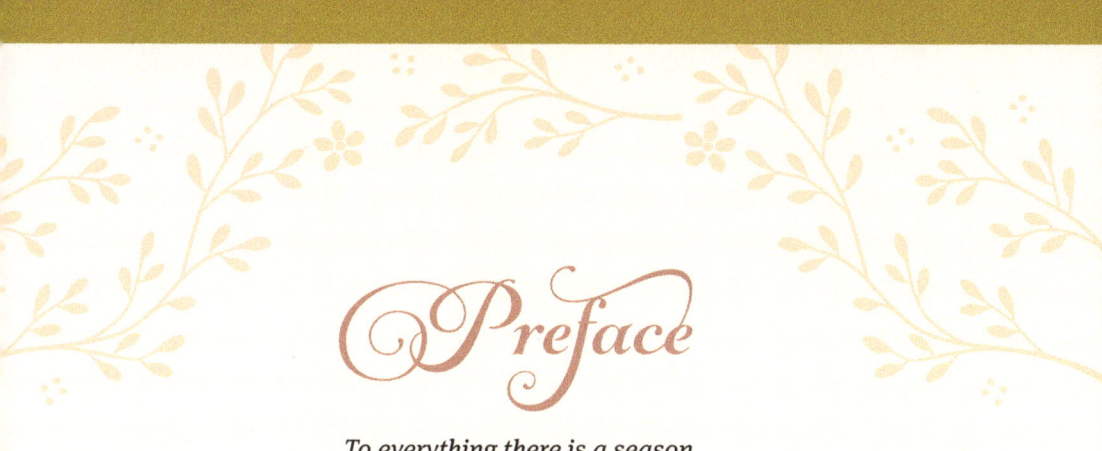

Preface

To everything there is a season,
a time for every purpose under heaven.

ECCLESIASTES 3:1 NKJV

As I SAT IN MY LIVING ROOM mesmerized by the bright embers glowing in the fireplace, I turned to look out the window and leaped to attention. Beautiful red cardinals filled a tree in my backyard. I had never seen so many in one place at a time. I sat motionless, afraid to move for fear they would fly away. My eyes welled up with tears of joy and sadness. The crimson birds against the blanket of snow were like a beacon of hope shining through the darkness I was feeling from the loss of my mother. I wondered if God had sent them to cheer me up, to remind me that my mother's pain and suffering had ended, and she was in a glorious place now. I could feel her presence, and it stirred something inside me. I became more aware that our days are numbered and if there is anything we need to say or want to accomplish, we'd better do it now before it's too late. I also felt the voice of God prompting me that it was time to write this book.

At that time, I worked as a registered nurse, assessing patients for insurance companies. As I listened to the medical history of my clients,

I was touched by the unconditional love, devotion, and heartache family members endured, as they became caregivers to someone who once cared for them. At the end of my visits, I wrote a detailed nurse's note and I was stunned when a care coordinator said, "I love receiving cases from you. I can't wait to read your summaries because it's like reading a story." That's when I realized my twenty-plus years as a nurse had been preparing me to become a writer.

As I pondered what my book would be about, I thought about the significant impact my great-aunt Dorothy Kinne had on my life. She was the one who inspired and set in motion my desire to write about moments in my life—that have potential to change somebody else's. She was like a surrogate grandmother to me since both my grandmothers died before I turned seventeen. I enjoyed visiting her and listening as she spoke of our heritage and how she overcame so many obstacles in her life. She survived the Great Depression, she ran her own screen-printing business, she knew the agony of losing a child, and she launched my love for birding as I watched her identify the birds in her backyard. Many years ago, she entered into the presence of the Lord, but the legacy she left behind will never be forgotten. *I don't think we realize the value of family stories until the person who told them is gone.* At the end of one of my visits with Aunt Dorothy, she handed me a *Guideposts* magazine. I was intrigued by the heartwarming true stories, and it sparked the idea of someday writing my own.

Everyone has a story, as unique as the person telling it. Sharing our stories helps us connect on a deeper level as we realize we are not alone in our struggles. I hope these stories give you peace and hope for the future knowing that nothing comes into our lives without a purpose. Every heartache, struggle, and triumph leads us closer to God and closer to the person we were meant to be.

With love and blessings,
Judy Julien

Introduction

My plans aren't your plans, nor are your ways my ways, says the LORD. Just as the heavens are higher than the earth, so are my ways higher than your ways, and my plans than your plans.

ISAIAH 55:8–9 CEB

I LOVED LISTENING to my parents and grandparents tell stories about their journeys through life. Those stories never got old, no matter how many times I heard them. It was as if I was listening to a walking history book of my family's heritage. I realized those stories would eventually fade away if they weren't written down. When my mother passed away, that was it—her book was finished but there were stories of her life I had never heard, and I felt as though a part of my heritage seemed to float away like the smoke of a blown-out candle.

I am on a mission to inspire people to tell their stories because we never know the impact they can have on someone else's life. We have the power to encourage and change lives by sharing how God has brought us through difficult times. Sometimes our journey takes us down a straight and narrow road, but unexpectedly, we may face sharp curves and rough terrain, prompting us to ask the question, *Why is this happening? Where is God?* Even though we may not understand, we can still trust God to know what is best for us.

I believe we have divine appointments ordained by God so He can accomplish His work through us. We're all on a journey to be the person God wants us to be. Every situation we face causes us to grow and become more like Him.

My prayer is for anyone reading this to be encouraged, knowing you are not alone. When you read this, I hope you will discover how God is leading in your own life.

We can't see the whole picture because we see our lives through a short lens, but God has the wide-angle lens, and He knows what is best for us. May you find love and peace from whatever you are going through right now, as you experience the *grace to embrace* your journey while God is writing your story.

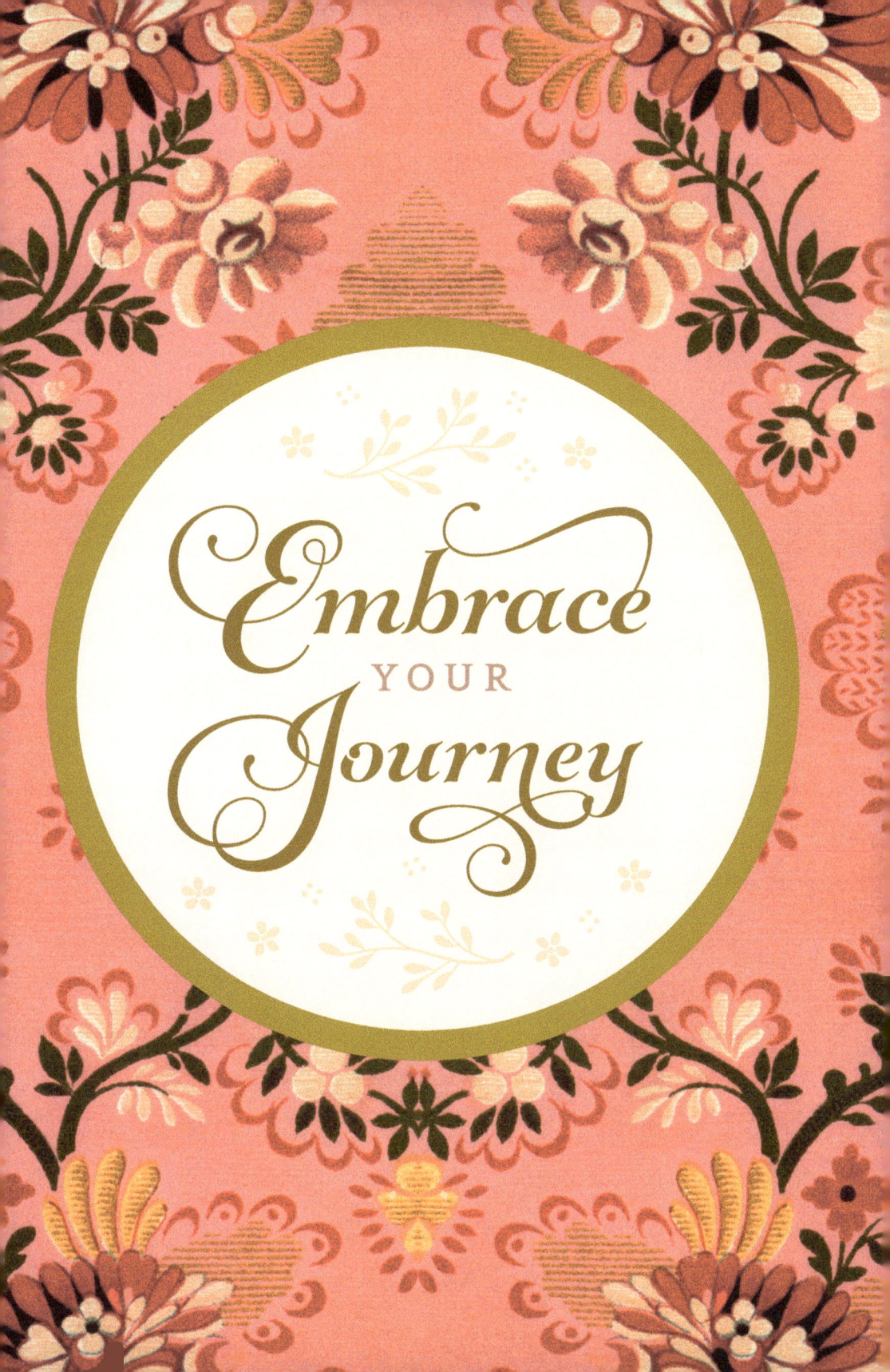

1
From Grace to Embrace

*"For I know the plans I have for you,"
declares the Lord, "plans to prosper you and not
to harm you, plans to give you hope and a future."*

JEREMIAH 29:11 NIV

MY WORLD SHATTERED when I received the call. A family friend said he'd heard that our seventeen-year-old daughter, Elizabeth, might be pregnant. He knew from the fact she was hiding it from us that she must be very frightened. I was in shock and felt numb. How could my daughter possibly be pregnant? Her classmates considered her a "Jesus freak!" She carried her Bible to school, wore T-shirts plastered with Bible verses, and prayed before eating her lunch in the cafeteria. I had spoken with her many times about saving herself until marriage. In fact, for her sixteenth birthday, I had helped her plant a white rosebush in the backyard to symbolize her virginity and as a reminder to keep herself pure until marriage. Why did this happen, and how could I have missed any signs of her pregnancy?

That evening, my husband knelt in front of Elizabeth and lovingly asked her if it was true. She admitted, "Yes, it's true, but I didn't want to tell you because you'd be disappointed in me." My husband enveloped her in his arms and told her we loved her and would do everything we could to help her. My heart ached for her and the baby she was carrying. I knew her life of fun and adventure would soon be replaced with nighttime feedings, dirty diapers, and adult responsibilities. Many questions began running through my mind: *Would she be a single parent? Who is the dad? Would he be in the picture, or will this baby grow up without a father? Would I be the one raising this baby?* My heart was broken knowing that she had been enduring this burden on her own, afraid of what our reaction might be.

On our first visit to the obstetrician, when we heard that precious little heartbeat for the first time, I instantly fell in love with the tiny blessing that would make me a grandmother. My sorrow quickly turned into joy as we began preparing for this precious yet unexpected gift from God, who would be loved no matter the circumstances surrounding her conception.

On a warm spring day when the world was bringing forth new life, I became a grandmother to the most beautiful baby girl I had ever seen. Mariah Elizabeth had a head full of soft brown hair, chubby little cheeks,

and dimples that melted my heart. I will never forget the pride, love, and joy I felt holding that precious gift from God.

Sometimes our lives don't turn out the way we had planned or expected. Instead of focusing on what could have been—on lost dreams, heartache, and pain—focus on the truth of knowing that God is in control of our journey and His ways are higher than ours.

My husband and I showed our daughter *grace*, and we *embraced* the bend in the road, knowing God was in control. We don't always know how God will work things out in our lives, but we can trust Him to finish writing our story.

*Children are a gift from the L ORD;
they are a reward from him.*

PSALM 127:3 NLT

2
I Believe in Miracles

*He performs wonders that cannot be fathomed,
miracles that cannot be counted.*

JOB 5:9

SHE HAD DEMENTIA and hadn't spoken for over a year. She was a resident in the Alzheimer's unit at a nursing facility where I trained certified nurse assistants. I sat down at the table where she had just finished her lunch. One of the workers came over and said, "Helen [not her real name] used to sing in the choir at her church." I gently asked, "Do you want to sing something with me, Helen?" No response. Easter was only a few days away, so I began singing an old familiar hymn, "In the Garden," to see if she would respond. *"I come to the garden alone, while the dew is still on the roses . . ."* To everyone's surprise, Helen began singing along. She knew every word better than I, and she sang all four verses, word for word. There wasn't a dry eye in the room as we witnessed the miracle of Helen singing this beautiful old hymn.

A few years later, I was rummaging through a closet and found an old cassette tape. I popped it into a player and my eyes welled up with tears as I heard my deceased grandfather singing in a men's quartet. His deep bass voice, along with my dad's baritone, blended perfectly with the four-part harmony. I was instantly transported to my past, sitting in a church pew, listening to the gospel quartet. The man singing melody had recently been placed in a memory care facility because he was suffering from dementia. The Holy Spirit put it on my heart to send the recording to his daughter. It had such a powerful impact on me, so I wanted to share it with her. I converted the song into digital format and emailed it to her. She was so thrilled; she quickly went to visit her dad so she could play it for him. When she arrived, her dad was very agitated and upset, which can be typical of dementia patients, but when she played the music, he immediately calmed down and began singing along, as if he had stepped back in time. It was a miracle how the music freed a memory that had been tangled up in the web of such an insidious disease. Ironically, the title of the song was *"I Believe in Miracles."*

My grandfather always spoke with dignity and grace with his deep, booming voice. He had studied the Scriptures for many years and could easily quote passages from memory. Sadly, a stroke left him physically handicapped the last twelve years of his life. Although he had been robbed of his physical strength, his faith remained strong, and he was still able to share his wisdom of God's Word because that area of his brain had been preserved. What a blessing that even though physical and mental abilities may become hindered, the Word of the Lord remains strong.

"The grass withers, the flower fades, but the word of our God will stand forever" (Isaiah 40:8 ESV). The Lord is good, time after time. He gives us hope through His Word, His Son, and the gift of music. I believe in miracles because I believe in God!

I will sing of the LORD's great love forever;
with my mouth I will make your faithfulness
known through all generations.

PSALM 89:1

3

Silver Lining

He who dwells in the shelter of the Most High will abide in the shadow of the Almighty. I will say to the Lord, "My refuge and my fortress, my God, in whom I trust."

PSALM 91:1–2 ESV

THE SIGNS WERE ALL THERE for a long time, but my father refused to see a doctor. My mother was concerned that Dad had been waking up with night sweats and assumed it was from their new flannel sheets. I urged her to get him to a doctor, but he kept refusing. After months of ignoring his symptoms, he began to lose his appetite and, consequently, lost a lot of weight. Finally, he went to see his physician, who began treating him for hyperparathyroidism. My dad continued to get weaker every day, so Mom called the doctor to convince him that something was terribly wrong. The physician referred my dad to a specialist, who could not see him for one month.

On the day of his appointment, Dad was so weak he had to use a wheelchair. Some friends drove him in their van, which would allow him to lie down for the one-hour trip because he was unable to sit up. The specialist took a brief look at my dad and said, "I need to do a biopsy of the lump in your neck, *right now*, under local anesthesia." After the procedure, we waited for the results. The physician came into the room, placed his hand on Dad's shoulder, and with sincere compassion gave us the news: "I'm sorry to have to tell you this, but you have lymphoma. I want you to go straight to the hospital to be admitted."

After more testing, my dad was diagnosed with stage 4 lymphoma. He began the rigorous chemotherapy treatments, which depleted his blood count. My husband, Mike, and I dropped Dad and Mom off at the hospital so Dad could get a blood transfusion, then we drove to a nearby mall so they could have some time alone. We stopped by a jewelry store and a necklace caught my eye. It had a light blue center stone with a shiny silver border. Mike bought it to cheer me up, then we drove to a park and sat on a bench overlooking the river. As I held the blue stone in my hand admiring its beauty in the sunlight, I thought to myself, *I wonder if Dad will survive this cancer*? I turned to Mike and asked, "Can you give me something to think about whenever I wear my necklace?"

Without missing a beat, he said, *"Every cloud has a silver lining!"*

That was perfect! After many months of chemotherapy and more blood transfusions, my dad went into total remission. We are so thankful for

God's healing and preservation. My necklace reminds me of the miraculous silver lining to Dad's cancer diagnosis.

Every time a dark cloud comes into our lives, we can trust God, knowing He is in control. Going through trials makes us stronger. We learn to trust God when all hope is gone, because it forces us to seek His help. It also equips us to help others who are going through similar struggles. When you go through the fire, you will come out a different person, changed and refined as the dross rises to the top to be discarded. God gives us *grace* so we can *embrace* our dark clouds, knowing there is a silver lining.

*But those who hope in the L*ORD *will renew their strength.*
They will soar on wings like eagles;
they will run and not grow weary, they
will walk and not be faint.
ISAIAH 40:31

4
The Blue Ridge Mountains

*In his hand are the depths of the earth,
and the mountain peaks belong to him.*

PSALM 95:4

I STOOD ALONE, gazing over the Blue Ridge Mountains, admiring the ethereal shades of blue that went on for miles in the distance. The mystical blue fog lingered over the forest below in layers, like a perfectly painted color wash blending into the sky. I listened in the silence, groping for any sound at all, but not even the wind could be heard. It was rare to be at an overlook alone, and the serenity washed over me like a cleansing flood, erasing all the stress from my mind. It was one of the most beautiful sights I had ever seen. The pure splendor surrounded me in unbroken perfection, and I whispered the name—*"Jesus"*—because I was overwhelmed with His presence. I felt like I was the only person on earth, alone with God and His beautiful masterpiece. The silence was broken by the sound of a branch snapping on the craggy slope. I wondered if it might be a black bear coming out to forage in the early evening hours. Just yesterday, a woman had spotted a mother bear with her cubs playing in a pool down the road from our hotel. I wondered if my fourth trip to Asheville would fulfill my dream of seeing a bear; however, it was still an elusive dream.

On this trip to the Blue Ridge Mountains I may not have seen a bear, but I was able to cross something else off of my bucket list—driving a muscle car on the Blue Ridge Parkway. My 2001 Z28 was unable to make the trip from Illinois, so I rented a convertible Camaro to fulfill my dream of driving a sports car on "America's Favorite Drive." It was the highlight of my trip as I drove along the winding, tree-lined road through the mountains. The scenery was spectacular, and with the top down, I had an unobstructed view of the hazy, blue mountains. With the wind in my hair and the sun on my face, the car hugged every curve along the road that gets millions of visitors every year. I stopped at a place called Craggy Gardens and got out of the car to enjoy the magnificent panoramic view. It was so unexpected to find myself alone at this popular lookout, enjoying a moment of solitude with the Creator. As the sun slowly inched its way to the horizon, cars arrived and people started gathering to admire the show-stopping bands of red, orange, yellow, and fuschia being painted across the sky. My brief, serendipitous encounter was over, but it will be etched in my mind forever.

Earlier that evening when I left our hotel on that journey up the mountain, I had taken a wrong turn, and instead of taking ten minutes to reach the parkway, it took me twenty, and I became agitated. I knew the sun would be setting soon and I wanted all of my time to be spent on the parkway rather than the bustling interstate. But when I got out of the car and found myself alone at the lookout, it was as if someone had flipped a switch, and time stood still. Nothing else mattered! God had completely changed my perspective, and all I could think of was Him. The majestic mountains reflected the majesty of the Creator and I was instantly filled with peace, tranquility, and the overwhelming presence of God.

And the peace of God,
which transcends all understanding,
will guard your hearts and your minds in Christ Jesus.
PHILIPPIANS 4:7

5

Jaws

*Therefore Death expands its jaws,
opening wide its mouth; into it will descend their
nobles and masses with all their brawlers and revelers.*

ISAIAH 5:14

MY UNCLE TED REED worked for Universal Studios. He drove an eighteen-wheeler that hauled props, cameras, and equipment used during filming. He also did some acting and was featured in *Knight Rider*, *A Few Good Men*, *The Horse Whisperer*, *The Blues Brothers*, *Jaws*, and *Jaws II*. He drove the DeLorean in *Back to the Future*, he drove a rig in *Smokey and the Bandit*, and rode a horse in *Far and Away* and he performed in many others. After filming *Jaws* in Martha's Vineyard, my uncle stopped at our house in Illinois on his way back to California. He traveled with a watchdog to keep thieves away from his truck. He got the dog shortly after filming *The Blues Brothers* in Chicago when eighty gallons of fuel was siphoned from his rig on the first night. The other truckers laughed at him for getting a dog, but it wasn't long before they all had dogs sitting in their cabs. His dog's name was Igor, an English Bull Terrier, generally docile but ready to engage should there be any trouble. We had a measly beagle named Fella and to avoid any conflict, we kept them apart by placing Igor in our fenced-in backyard while Fella stayed at a safe distance indoors. It wasn't long before Igor had chewed his way through the screen of our back door. We went outside to investigate, and somehow Fella got out and tried to nibble on Igor's food. Before we could stop him, Igor latched onto Fella's ear with a death grip and would *not* let go. We coaxed, we tugged, we demanded him to let go, but nothing worked. His teeth were like a steel trap, and he refused to release our poor dog, who stood motionless, in full submission. My uncle swiftly grabbed the hose and doused Igor's head, causing him to release Fella from his jaw. Luckily, his ear was left intact with only a minor injury.

How many times do we drop our guard and take our eyes off the Lord, only to let Satan take hold of our thoughts and desires? We begin to doubt, we get anxious, we feel numb, we slip away from the truth, and at times, we may feel abandoned. But no matter how far we slip away, God is faithful. He never leaves our side. He's always there, waiting for us to run back to His open arms. Don't let Satan get his grip on you. He wants to fill your mind with lies and trap you in your sin. Let go. Turn from your sin, and flee to Jesus. He never gives up on us. It doesn't matter what you've done or where you've been; He loves you and wants to change your life.

When Christ was dying on the cross between two criminals, one of the thieves turned to Him and said, "'Jesus, remember me when you come into your kingdom.' Jesus answered him, 'Truly I tell you, today you will be with me in paradise'" (Luke 23:42–43). The thief simply had to believe Jesus was the Son of God, and Christ guaranteed he would be in paradise that very day. Even in the midst of Jesus's suffering the most painful death, He still showed love and compassion to the very crowd who had beaten Him. He prayed, "Father, forgive them, for they know not what they do" (Luke 23:34 ESV).

There is no greater love—"Whoever does not love does not know God, because God is love" (1 John 4:8).

If you have never trusted Christ as your Savior, do it now before it's too late. Step away from Satan, and set yourself free from the bondage of your sin. Make that decision today; don't put it off, because none of us knows the hour or the day of our last breath, so be ready.

If you declare with your mouth, "Jesus is Lord,"
and believe in your heart that God raised
him from the dead, you will be saved.

ROMANS 10:9

6
A Father's Prayer

Thanks be to God for his indescribable gift!

2 CORINTHIANS 9:15

It was the day after Thanksgiving when I received a desperate call from my son John. He was concerned about his wife, Julie, who was thirty-two weeks pregnant with their first child. He explained that she'd been complaining of a headache and what felt like a tight band around her abdomen. Being a registered nurse, I knew exactly what it meant. I tried to stay calm without sending him into a panic. I told John he should take her to the hospital right away to get checked, just to be safe. It wasn't long before my suspicions were confirmed—the physician diagnosed her with HELLP syndrome, which is life threatening. Her blood pressure was dangerously elevated, her liver enzymes were off the chart, and her platelet count was so low she was in danger of spontaneously hemorrhaging. The nurse said she had never seen platelets that low before. She called the nearest hospital with a neonatal intensive care unit to send a helicopter. Delivery was the only way to save the lives of baby and mom.

The helicopter arrived, and the medical team transferred Julie onto the transport gurney. We took a moment and placed our hands on her as we gave a desperate prayer for God to protect her and the baby, then she was wheeled away by the life flight team. John asked me to drive him to the hospital, which was an hour away. As we drove down the interstate, the blinking helicopter lights in the night sky caught our attention. John felt so helpless because more than anything he wanted to be by his wife's side, holding her hand, and comforting her during this frightening ordeal. We watched in silence until the flashing red lights faded into the distance out of sight, then John softly whispered under his breath, "I can't raise this baby without her." As we drove to the level one trauma center where I had worked as a nurse, I gave John explicit directions so he could reach the labor and delivery unit as quickly as possible. I dropped him off at the entrance then proceeded to park in the deck.

The medical team explained to us what was about to happen, then they took Julie into the operating room. Family members on both sides gathered together, praying and pacing the floor, as we nervously waited for this precious, unsuspecting baby to be rudely snatched from his warm, safe haven two months too soon. Jacob weighed three pounds nine ounces and was so tiny you could see the veins through his translucent skin. The neonatal team worked swiftly as they stimulated his delicate little body, encouraging him to breathe on his own. He was blue and limp. My son turned away because he didn't want to watch his son die. As he prayed with a father's heart, God heard him and breathed life into Jacob's premature lungs. The neonatal team rushed him to the NICU where he was hooked up to monitors and placed in a warm, sterile isolette. A feeding tube was placed down his nose because he was too weak to nurse or take a bottle.

It was a long road, but after four long weeks, Jacob was strong enough to go home. Weighing a little over five pounds, he was discharged a few days before Christmas. God responded to my son's prayer in the delivery room, fully relating to what John was feeling, for God himself turned away when His only Son died on the cross as He took on the sins of the world. I'm sure He felt the pain of a father with true empathy and mercy.

Jacob is our little miracle, and he brings us so much joy. It was an extra special Christmas that year, and we thanked God for giving us such a wonderful blessing. As we held our tiny bundle of joy, we reflected on another miracle—the birth of Christ; the Messiah who was born in a filthy, unsterile stable, with no skilled physicians on hand to safely bring Him into this world. That Christmas, we praised God for the gift of His Son and for the gift of our precious Jacob.

For nothing will be impossible with God.

LUKE 1:37 ESV

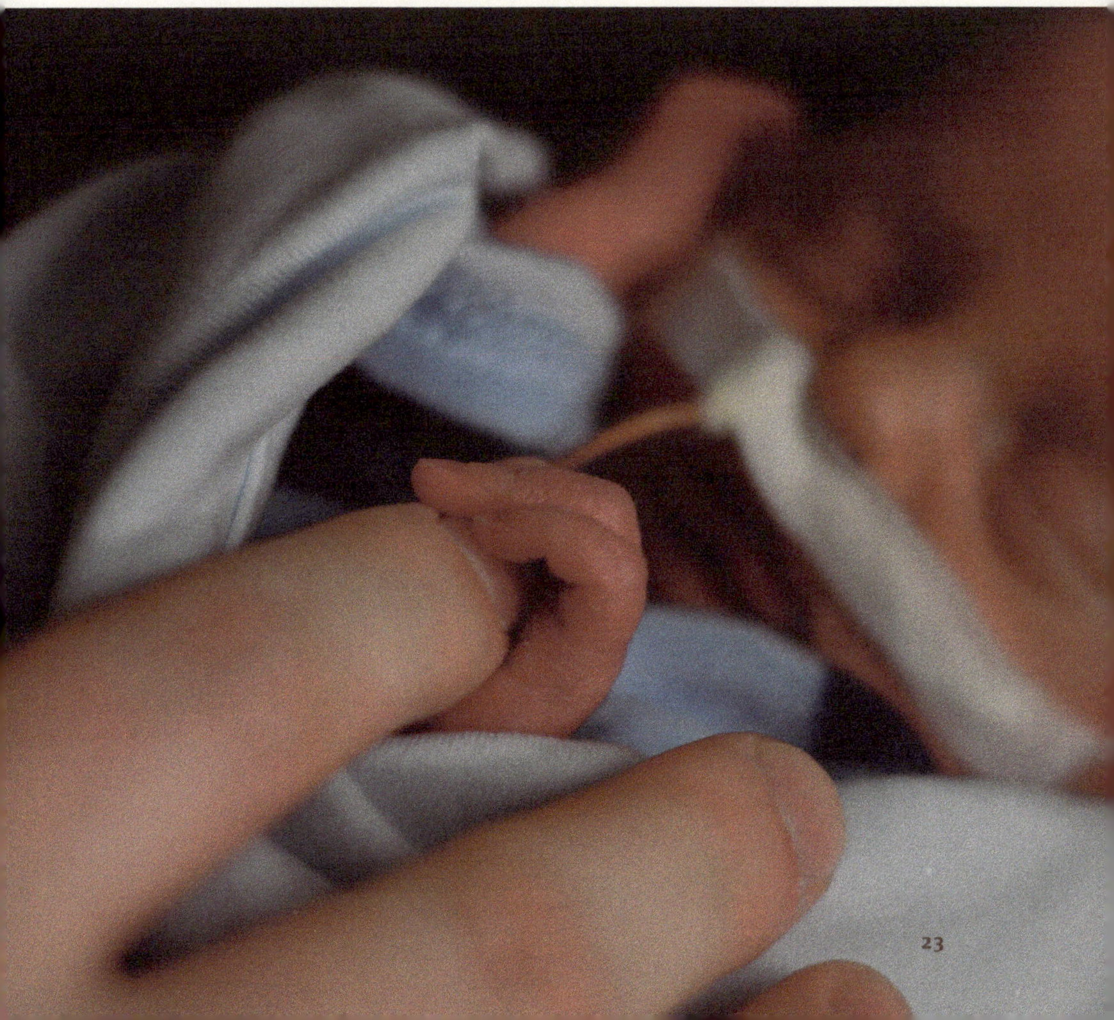

7
Masterpiece

All things were made through him, and without him was not any thing made that was made.

JOHN 1:3 ESV

I SAT AT THE EASEL with an HB pencil in my hand and began sketching faint lines of the still life in my art class. I drew an outline of the figure, then filled in some details before adding the shadows of light being cast onto the subject. The soothing violin concerto softly played in the background, calming my mind as I struggled to capture the likeness of the objects. After a sufficient amount of time, the other students and I paused and walked around the room to admire each other's work; each rendition was a true masterpiece.

My entire life I dreamt of being an artist. I don't know why, it just sounded glamorous to be able to create something from nothing. I envisioned having an art studio on the second floor of my home, with an easel by the window overlooking the beautiful mountains. I embraced those desires and took my first art class at the age of fifty-eight—because it's never too late to learn something new and fulfill a dream. When I'm drawing, it's as if time stands still and nothing else matters; it's therapy for my mind, body, and soul.

I'm so grateful for my art teacher, who opened my eyes and helped me discover a part of myself I didn't know existed. I may not have an art studio overlooking the mountains, but I have a desk in the corner of my office. Since I began this new journey, a few of my grandchildren have shown an interest, and they enjoy sitting at my desk, creating something beautiful. I love to watch their self-expressions flow onto the paper while they create something unique and as precious as the child painting it.

God designed each of us as a one-of-a-kind creation. Before we were formed in our mother's womb, He knew us. We are the masterpiece of His creative mind, and He has His divine signature on every one of us. I'm in awe of God's power displayed in the majestic mountains, the spectacular sunsets, or the mysterious rings orbiting Saturn. It takes me hours just to draw a simple figure, but He didn't have to spend hours coming up with an idea and He didn't have to stand back staring at his canvas contemplating

the next brush stroke. It's impossible to comprehend His infinite power. We are part of His design (Psalm 139:13), and He knows us better than we know ourselves.

The night before Jesus was crucified, the soldiers came to arrest Him. When Christ asked whom they were seeking, they said, "Jesus of Nazareth." Jesus replied, "I AM He," and they drew back and fell to the ground (John 18:6). The God of all creation stood before them, and when He spoke His name, "I Am," the soldiers felt the power of the almighty God merely by His voice. We are His work of art, a true masterpiece.

For we are God's masterpiece. He has created us anew in Christ Jesus, so we can do the good things he planned for us long ago.

EPHESIANS 2:10 NLT

8

Christmas Is a Time for Giving

*Whoever is generous to the poor lends to the
LORD, and he will repay him for his deed.*

PROVERBS 19:17 ESV

I WAS EIGHT YEARS OLD when my mother announced, "There won't be as many gifts for Christmas this year." The factory where my dad worked had been on strike, so money was tight. She was preparing my three siblings and me for a disappointing Christmas. The thought of receiving fewer gifts concerned me a bit, but not as much as the anguish I could see on my mother's face. On Christmas morning, after we opened our gifts, she held up her hands and confessed, "That's it!" I felt sorry for her. Of course, I was disappointed as any child would be, but more than anything, I just wanted to wrap my arms around her because I could tell she was upset. I'm sure she did her best to make the little money she had stretch among four children. I don't remember my parents opening any gifts to each other that year. They had sacrificed to give us more.

Many years later, with a family of our own, my husband and I were in a similar situation. Mike was working only part time while going to college full time, and we didn't have extra money to buy our two children Christmas gifts. I went to my parents' home and rummaged through the attic in search of toys from my childhood. It was like a flea market up there since nobody in our family threw anything away. I found a doll bed, a doll highchair, and a Suzy Homemaker oven for my daughter. I discovered a baseball bat and glove from my mother's childhood, and she said I could have it for my son. As my husband and I were intending to present these used toys to our unsuspecting children, God had another plan. A few days before Christmas, a letter arrived in the mail with a check for one hundred dollars. A generous man from our church had sent it, though we had never mentioned our financial struggles to him. It was such a blessing to be able to buy gifts for our precious children. We took the last bit of money and purchased a Christmas ornament, symbolizing the kindness shown to us. Every year we faithfully place the ornament on our tree as a reminder that *Christmas is a time for giving*.

Sometimes we get so caught up in the gifts that we lose sight of the reason we celebrate Christmas. God gave us His most prized possession, His only Son. I wonder how Joseph must have felt, not being able to provide a clean, safe, suitable place for Mary to deliver their son. And not just any son, but the Messiah, the King of Kings and Lord of Lords, who came to save His people from their sins. He left His heavenly throne and entered the world in a lowly stable. He was God's gift to us; He is the gift of eternal life for those who will accept Him as their Savior. So if you haven't opened your gift yet, unwrap His free gift and claim it because it's the greatest gift you will ever receive.

And this is the record, that God hath given us eternal life, and this life is in his Son.

1 JOHN 5:11 KJV

9
The Comfort of Cardinals

Blessed are those who mourn, for they will be comforted.

MATTHEW 5:4

NOT LONG AFTER MY MOTHER DIED, beautiful red cardinals filled a tree just outside my window. I didn't think it was too unusual, since I live in the Midwest and they frequently stop by for some black oil sunflower seeds. It was unusual, though, that I counted twelve of them, sitting in a tree, taking turns at my feeder. The bright red males stood out against the pearly, white snow, and the females' vibrant coral beaks were a stunning vision of beauty. I was grieving from the loss of my mother, but the birds cheered me up as I watched them from my sofa.

A few months later, the cardinals were still happily sitting in my tree when I left for work. As I was walking along with one of the other nurses, I mentioned how I was still mourning the loss of my mother. She stopped, turned to me, and said, "You know, some people say when you see a cardinal or a butterfly, it means a visitor from heaven is nearby."

I was stunned. I hadn't even mentioned the birds to her. My eyes welled up with tears as I told her, "The tree in my backyard has been filled with cardinals these past few months." I thought it was a bit unusual, but I didn't think of it as a sign from heaven. I asked what prompted her to share that with me. She shrugged and said, "I don't know. I just felt like I should say it."

I have read stories of people claiming to experience visitors from heaven when they feel down or are missing someone, but I was skeptical until it happened to me. God has a way of cheering us up when we need it, and the brilliant red cardinals certainly did lift my spirits. I don't know if it's possible to have visitors from heaven, but when I see a cardinal in my backyard, it will always remind me of my mother, and give me comfort knowing she is in heaven.

Losing my mother broke my heart. The intense anguish I felt blindsided me. But God, in His mercy, comforted me with the crimson visitors and gave me peace. Red was my mother's favorite color. She loved wearing red, she loved red roses, and she loved her red car. I take comfort knowing my mom isn't suffering anymore. Not long before she passed away, she told me, "I'm ready to go," because she knew she was going to meet her Lord and Savior.

Cardinals

I looked out my window and in the tree
Were bright red cardinals looking at me.
A visitor from heaven, did it mean you are near?
I felt you were watching, and saying, "I'm here."
My heart was afflicted, overwhelmed with grief
But the birds gave me comfort and sweet relief.
God in his mercy filled me with peace.
The birds a reminder, your suffering had ceased.
My heart felt your presence and loving embrace,
I knew you were home in a beautiful place.

J. J.

For you have been my help,
and in the shadow of your wings I will sing for joy.

PSALM 63:7 ESV

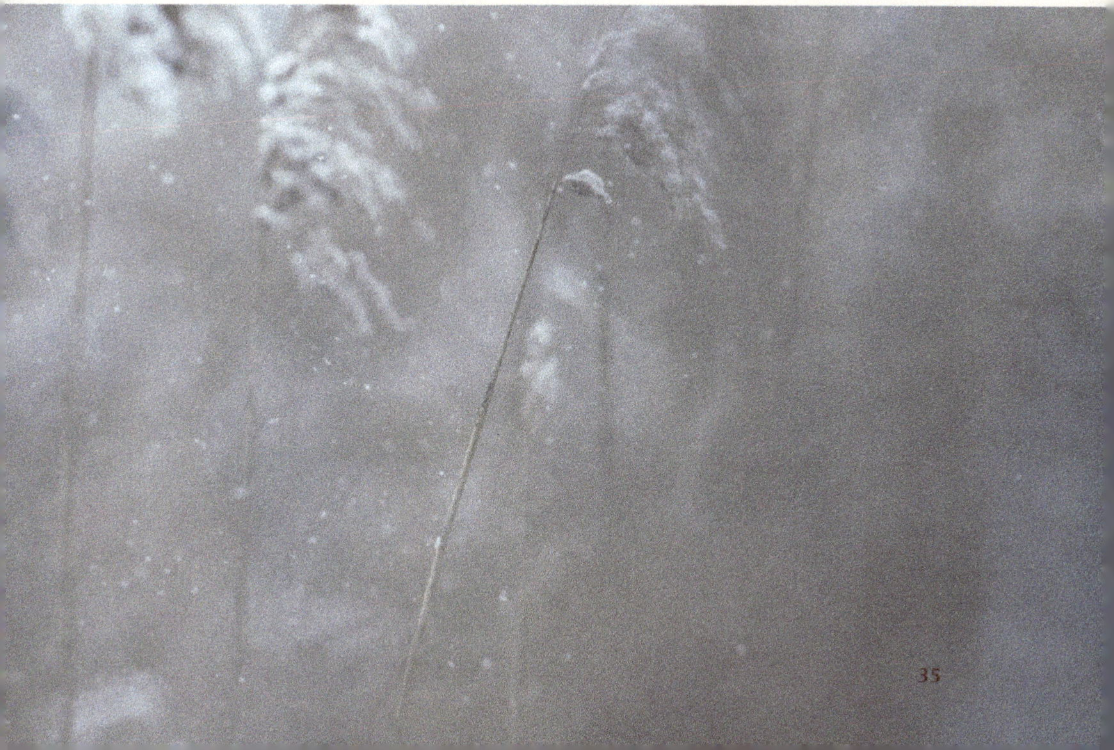

10
The Wedding

And now these three remain:
faith, hope and love.
But the greatest of these is love.
1 CORINTHIANS 13:13 ESV

"**LET'S JUST ELOPE!**" I blurted out in exasperation. It was early March of 1980 and Mike and I were planning a June wedding, but his mother would not give us her blessing, and we had to put everything on hold. She thought we were too young and thought it would be in our best interest for Mike to finish college so we could have a better start. We were one year out of high school and had very low wage jobs, so money was going to be tight, but it didn't matter to us. We were head over heels in love and wanted to spend the rest of our lives together. I had already picked out my bridal gown and had started to plan what would be the best day of my life. We were crushed, but also determined not to let this roadblock prevent us from getting hitched. We didn't want to wait another year. We were scared and didn't know what to do. We also knew planning a wedding without her consent would be very stressful and complicated. Unfortunately, our reckless love caused us to make an irrational, impulsive decision. I didn't know it at the time, but I was about to do something I would later regret.

Several years after we eloped, I began to loathe going to weddings because they were a reminder of what I had given up. Every time I watched a bride make her entrance in her glamorous wedding gown I felt remorse, because I would never know how that moment felt. Mike would always reach for my hand and give it a squeeze, unsure if my tears were from the bride's beauty or because I regretted giving up the wedding of my dreams. He could sense my anguish and he wanted to put an end to my grief once and for all.

On March 4, 2003, Mike took me to a fancy restaurant for lunch. After we finished eating, he got up from the table and suddenly dropped to his knee. I thought he had fallen and bent down to help him. So did the waiter, who kept asking if he was all right. My husband stayed on one knee, motioning with his arm in the air, shooing the waiter away and reassuring him he was fine. Then Mike held up a shiny, past-present-future diamond ring and said, "Judy, my love for you grows deeper every day. Will you renew your vows with me so you can have the wedding of your dreams?" I took his head in my hands, and with tears in my eyes, kissed him, "yes," kiss, "yes," kiss, "yes!" I was ecstatic and began preparations right away. I chose a white, strapless gown covered in Swarovski crystals, a chapel-length veil, white, satin gloves, and a sparkling headpiece. My

bouquet was filled with pink sweet peas, blush roses, and tiny crystals. We invited one hundred guests, reserved a ballroom, and took dance lessons for our first dance, which was magical. Our amazing celebration was like something out of a fairy tale, and it was the happiest day of our lives, worth every single penny! Oh, and by the way, when the doors of the church opened, I took his breath away, but there were no tears.

Our vow renewal healed my regretful, wounded heart and gave me a new appreciation for weddings. I fell head over heels in love again, with the man of my dreams who made my dream come true. Not long after we eloped, Mike's mother apologized and became very dear to my heart. Unfortunately, she had passed away ten years before our vow renewal, but we had placed a yellow rose in her honor at the altar. It was an extravagant celebration for sure, but we realized when you place great value on something or *someone*, the investment of time and devotion is priceless.

Be devoted to one another in love.
Honor one another above yourselves.
ROMANS 12:10

11
Grandmother's Porch Swing

*My children, our love should not be just words and talk;
it must be true love, which shows itself in action.*

1 JOHN 3:18 GNT

WHEN I WAS A LITTLE GIRL, I loved sitting on the porch swing at my great-grandmother's house. Her real name was Grandma Reed but we called her Grandma Bird because she loved to sing. On rainy days my siblings and I would sit on the porch swing mesmerized by the percussion of raindrops tapping on the leaves. The gentle swaying motion soothed my soul, and I thought to myself, *Nothing in life could be better than this*! I would watch the cars swish by on the wet pavement as I watched a blue jay or chickadee in the nearby pine tree. I sat on that swing without a care in the world, and life was good.

It was always an adventure at grandma's Arts and Craft style home. We would explore her attic for old treasures or sit in the parlor listening to her stories of long ago. There was an old water pump by the back door, and we would take turns cranking the handle up and down until water gushed from the spout. Grandma had an orchard out back, the full length of her yard. We would help her collect apricots, apples, and grapes so she could make jams and juices. My mom and grandma spent hours in the kitchen canning apricots and making apricot and grape jelly. The tantalizing scent of the freshly pressed grape juice would always beckon me to the kitchen for a sample.

   I loved visiting my grandmother. She always had freshly baked chocolate drop cookies and plenty of hiding places for a great game of hide and seek. But the best part of visiting her was time spent on the front porch swing, watching the birds and lulling myself into a state of total relaxation. I wonder if my love for spa music and meditation began on my grandmother's porch swing, while my loving mother helped her in the kitchen.

My mom was a great example of what it means to honor God by serving and helping my grandmother through the harvest. Those memories created at her home are like priceless treasures in my heart. I hope I can place treasures in the hearts of my grandchildren that will continue through generations to come.

And whatever you do, in word or in deed, do everything in the name of the Lord Jesus, giving thanks to God the Father through him. COLOSSIANS 3:17 ESV

12
Bucket List Terror

*But seeing the wind, he became frightened,
and beginning to sink, he cried out, "Lord, save me!"*

MATTHEW 14:30 NASB

WHEN I WAS A YOUNG GIRL, an insolent boy pushed me into the deep end of the public pool. I didn't know how to swim, but luckily, my feet hit the bottom with enough force to push myself back to the surface, coughing and sputtering. That was the day I developed an unhealthy fear of deep water. Forty-five years later, I'm not sure why, I put jet skiing on my bucket list, despite my irrational phobia of being in deep water. I thought speeding across the water with the wind in my face would be exciting. My aunt owned some Jet Skis at her beautiful home on Marco Island, and she graciously let us stay for a few days. Our master suite had a balcony with breathtaking views of the sunrise. It's not every day you get to enjoy a private pool, hot tub, and beautiful lanai while on holiday! It was a dream vacation full of fond memories, but laced with terror on the Gulf of Mexico.

The day arrived for my cousin, Michelle, to take my husband, Mike, and me jet skiing. With Mike sitting behind me, I was the driver and we set out slowly, gliding along through the no-wake zone. We floated past elaborate million-dollar homes as some dolphins escorted us out to sea. I felt so free on the calm water in the canal. It was wonderful, and I loved it until I looked ahead and caught sight of the churning waves, just outside the no-wake zone. My heart started racing, my grip got tighter, and I could feel the adrenaline pumping through my veins. As soon as we were out of the no-wake-zone, Michelle yelled, "Let's go!" With much trepidation, I gave it a little gas. At first, it was exhilarating. Then, a speedboat raced past us, causing a huge wave to toss our Jet Ski up and down like a teeter-totter. I let off the gas thinking we were going to tip over. Mike yelled over my shoulder, "Turn into the wave!" This went on and on until we were miles from shore. The free feeling I had earlier quickly transformed into an enormous panic attack. The fear took control of my mind and I imagined hungry sharks in the water and me being tossed in for their dinner. The boats kept coming at us, and the waves got taller. I started screaming to Michelle, "Stop!" but by this time, she was yards ahead of me, unable to hear my pathetic pleas. My poor, innocent husband helplessly tried to calm me down. The speedboats were coming from all directions, terrorizing me with huge waves, and I was sure I'd meet my demise with one more four-foot wake. I stopped and let off the throttle, paralyzed as the waves tossed us up and down, while Mike's futile attempts failed to console me. Michelle noticed my distress and came over to investigate. Suddenly, I spotted a gray fin beginning to circle us. I screamed, pulling my legs up in sheer terror as my panic turned into hysteria. My sweet, patient cousin calmly reassured me, "Don't worry, that is a dolphin. Sharks' fins are straight, and that one is curved." As Mike and Michelle waited for me to regain my composure, I noticed my fair skin was beginning to burn despite applying sunscreen. I was so relieved when we finally headed back to the safety of Marco Island.

That experience reminded me of Peter walking on water to get to Jesus. When Peter stopped trusting, he became frightened and began to sink. I lost faith that the Jet Ski would keep me from tipping over into the shark-infested waters. (And just so you know, my fears weren't totally unfounded. Two days later, I overheard a woman telling someone she had been parasailing and the waters were filled with hammerhead sharks.)

How many times do we rely on our own strength to get us out of predicaments rather than have faith in God to keep us safe? Fear is the opposite of faith. Fear is not from God. Second Timothy 1:7 says, "For God has not given us a spirit of fear and timidity, but of power, love, and self-discipline" (NLT). The storms of life can cause us to become anxious but if we keep our eyes on the Lord, He will replace our fears with faith.

Fear not, for I am with you; be not dismayed,
for I am your God; I will strengthen you, I will help you,
I will uphold you with my righteous right hand.

ISAIAH 41:10 ESV

13
A Heart of Gold

Therefore be imitators of God, as beloved children.

EPHESIANS 5:1 ESV

HE LIVED JUST DOWN THE STREET in an old, dilapidated house. I didn't know his name or anything about him, but my ten-year-old self could tell he was very poor. Sometimes I would see him working in his yard when I rode my bike past his house. His clothes were old and tattered, and his face long and worn, resembling crinkled up parchment paper. He always gave me a slight smile when we made eye contact, so I knew he was kind. I imagined he was one hundred years old because of the way he wobbled when he walked with his cane.

My mom had a soft heart for the needy because her family didn't have much when she was growing up. Her mother was very frugal and would buy fifty-pound bags of flour because it was cheaper to buy in bulk. The bags were made of a cotton floral print, and when the flour was used up, my grandmother would take the material and transform it into a dress for my mother. In the early 1940s, neither of my parents knew the luxury of having indoor plumbing. They used a chamber pot and a shabby outhouse, or privy. Both my parents were born shortly after the Great Depression, so they knew firsthand what life was like to do without.

When my mother became aware of the poor gentleman down the street, she had compassion and wanted to do something nice for him. It was almost Thanksgiving, so she decided she would fill a box full of food and take it over to him. She wanted to add something extra special, so she baked one of her famous pumpkin pies. Whenever she baked one of her pies, the familiar scent of cinnamon and allspice filled the house, which always meant Thanksgiving would soon be here.

After loading up the goodies, we drove to the poor man's home. We knocked on the door and waited. We knew he didn't walk very fast, so we stood there for a little while. When he finally opened the door, his eyes lit up as he gazed at the freshly baked pie. His lips parted as a slight smile formed across his careworn face and he motioned for us to come in. His house was cold and bare, with furniture from another era. A cat sat on his kitchen table, licking his paws, ignoring us as if we weren't there. The old man's eyes welled up with tears, and his nose began to run. He reached for the handkerchief in his back pocket and thanked us profusely in a gravelly, breathy voice. He smiled at me, nodding his head in approval. My little heart melted with joy as I experienced for the first time what it meant to give to the poor.

That day my mom taught me a valuable lesson: to look beyond myself, to help those less fortunate, and to show God's love to others. She became more than just a mom to me that day. I put her on a pedestal as my hero and the most wonderful person I had ever known. Her love for the Lord made her rich because she had a heart of gold.

Sometimes we get so busy with our daily activities that we forget to notice the hurting people around us. When Christ ministered on earth, He never thought of Himself. He spent His days healing, feeding, teaching, and showing love, mercy, and grace to everyone, including His enemies. My mother's legacy was not in the things she left behind but in her example of how to love people and give generously to those less fortunate. I knew she loved the Lord because it was evident in her life. She blessed the man down the road, and I was blessed by her example. When we take the focus off ourselves and serve others, we receive a blessing in return. Christ came to serve, and He blesses us so we are able to bless others.

If among you, one of your brothers should become poor, in any of your towns within your land that the LORD your God is giving you, you shall not harden your heart or shut your hand against your poor brother.

DEUTERONOMY 15:7 ESV

14

Adoption

Defend the weak and the fatherless;
uphold the cause of the poor and the oppressed.

PSALM 82:3

I NEVER IMAGINED I would adopt. I already had two biological children, a beautiful blonde girl and a rambunctious redheaded boy. My children were nine and ten years old when I began to yearn for another baby to hold. I decided to become a foster mom so I could care for precious newborns waiting to be adopted. After six months of training, I finally received my foster license and began the waiting game for a placement.

One year went by with no calls from the agency, and I was beginning to wonder if I would ever get a baby to love. Then an unexpected call came the first week in January. When I answered it, I heard the words I had longed to hear: "We have a baby who needs a home." I was so excited! Finally, the wait was over. The caseworker went on, "It's a girl, six days old, and she is still in the nursery at the hospital." My heart ached for this precious baby. I didn't even know her, and already I wanted to hold her in my arms, kiss her, and love her as my own. The caseworker went on, "This baby is not waiting for adoption, and it won't be a short stay. She tested positive for cocaine; it will be a long-term placement." Her words floated in one ear and out the other. Even though I had originally planned on taking short-stay placements, the thought of a baby lying in the hospital with no parents broke my heart. I immediately felt a bond with her, like a mother who bonds with her unborn baby the moment she learns she is pregnant.

I told the caseworker I would affirm with my husband at work and call her right back. Mike didn't hesitate. He said, "Of course we'll take her." My heart was racing as I called the caseworker and exclaimed, "We'll take her!" I hung up the phone and immediately began thanking God and praying for this little blessing that needed me. I felt she was a gift from God, just like my first two children. When the precious little girl, wrapped in a hospital receiving blanket, was placed in my arms, it was love at first sight. I instantly bonded with my new daughter, Abigail Grace. She was so beautiful with dark hair and tan skin. On my way home, something changed inside me, and I emotionally became Abby's mother. I remember taking her out of the car, looking at her beautiful face, and saying, "Thank you, God, for placing her in my care, and please Lord, let me keep her."

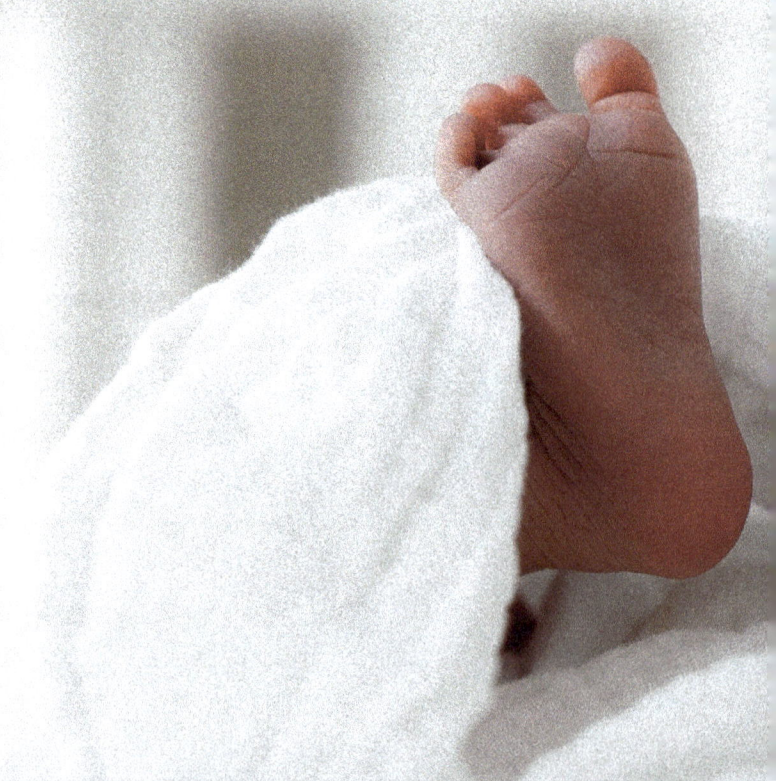

Three years later God answered that prayer, and we were able to adopt Abigail. One year after that, we took in baby Hannah and later we were able to adopt her too. It wasn't my plan, but God knew I loved babies and would accept His call for me to adopt. If I had received a baby right away instead of having to wait one year, I might not have taken a long-term placement. I believe the wait is what changed my heart. God's timing is always perfect, even when it means *not yet*. Once Abigail was placed in my arms, I didn't want to let her go.

Sometimes God calls us to reach beyond ourselves and do things we would never dream of doing. His plans are higher than ours. God changed my heart, and I experienced the blessings and joy of saying yes to adoption.

Religion that is pure and undefiled before God the Father is this: to visit orphans and widows in their affliction.

JAMES 1:27 ESV

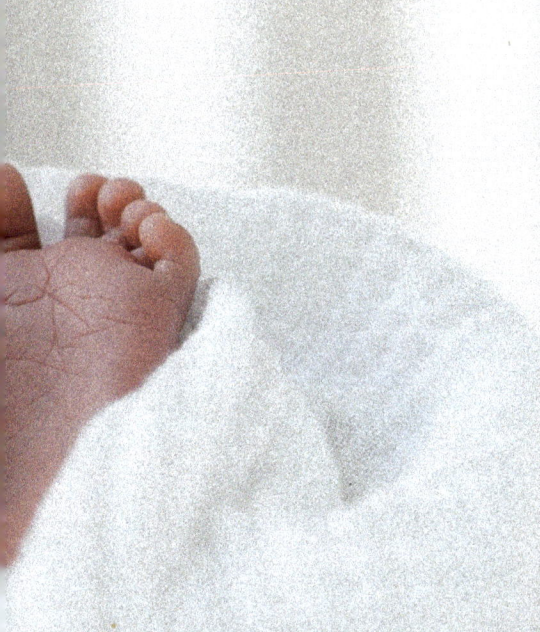

15

Dinner at Grandma's

*I will give thanks to the Lord with my whole heart;
I will recount all of your wonderful deeds.*

PSALM 9:1 ESV

SOME OF MY FONDEST childhood memories are going to my Grandma Lott's home for dinner. Every holiday we would extend tables from the dining room into the living room to accommodate our large family. The kitchen was usually bustling with aunts and uncles helping to prepare the meal. When I was very young I would play in the living room until dinner was ready. I still remember my excitement when I heard the buzz of the electric knife as Grandpa carved the turkey, because that meant it was almost time to eat. To this day, the sound of an electric knife transports me back to my grandparents' home. As I got a little older, I would stand next to the stove, out of everyone's way, mesmerized by the organized chaos of preparing all the food. I watched in amazement as the adults worked in perfect harmony gathering serving dishes, filling them with food and like a well-orchestrated symphony, the meal came together ready to be devoured. I remember as if it were yesterday, how proud I felt the first time my grandma asked me to stir the gravy. I can still feel her standing behind me, her hand on mine as she lovingly demonstrated the proper tempo to stir with a wooden spoon. She made the most delicious food, and I felt like royalty eating with real silver utensils, on her best china, at the table draped with her finest linen tablecloth.

After dinner, we'd gather the dirty dishes and pile them on the kitchen counter, then form an assembly line to wash them by hand because there was no electric dishwasher. Someone would wash as two or more people dried, then the beautiful, delicate, china was carefully returned to its safe place in the hutch. When the kitchen was back to its original order, we would gather in the living room to reminisce for many hours.

There was never a shortage of stories, especially from my uncles who often retold about the time they drove too fast around a curve in the country and wrecked the car. Or about the time they had just moved into an Arts and Craft style home and discovered a hidden coat closet, which was part of the oak paneling under the main floor stairs. They hid inside and jumped out to scare Grandma and were severely punished by my grandfather. The story that always got a good laugh was the time Grandpa was carrying a chamber pot to the outhouse in mid-winter and slipped on the ice. He quickly threw the pot as far as he could into the snow before falling to the ground.

My dad had a ton of stories; in fact, he will go down in history as the king of storytelling. I loved to hear him talk about my great-grandpa Duncan, because I never knew him since he died before I was born. My dad helped Grandpa Duncan milk the cows on his farm, then deliver cream to the creamery in Bloomington, Illinois, which is currently my hometown.

Listening to those stories was like a step back in time, and a reminder of how thankful I am for indoor plumbing.

I will always cherish time spent at my grandmother's house, where I learned the importance of spending time with family, and how to work as a team in the kitchen. When I was in high school, my grandmother was diagnosed with cancer, and it wasn't long before it spread to other parts of her body and insidiously ended her life. I adored and admired her with all of my being. She was a gentle, quiet, loving person, and I never saw her lose her temper, not even once. She never complained about the pain that ravaged through her body, as cancer took its toll. I was so enamored by her courage, and I hope I can emulate her with my own life. Sometimes things are taught, and sometimes things are caught.

We never know the impact our lives have on those around us. It's a great responsibility to live a Christ-centered life, knowing our children and grandchildren are watching us. Our behavior and choices today could affect the lives of generations to come. I feel very blessed to have these treasured family memories, where I learned that time is short but memories are for a lifetime.

*You shall teach them diligently to your children,
and shall talk of them when you sit in your house
and when you walk by the way, and when
you lie down, and when you rise up.*
DEUTERONOMY 6:7 ESV

16
Home Alone

*Save me from my enemies,
my God; protect me from those who attack me!*

PSALM 59:1 GNT

My sister and I were home alone one evening when we heard a knock at the front door. I was thirteen, and my sister Jennifer was nine. I ran to open it, expecting to see a friend, but instead a man was standing on the porch holding a vacuum cleaner. He asked, "Can I talk to your mom or dad? I'm selling these vacuums." My heart started racing. I didn't know what to say because I didn't want him to know we were home alone. I wished I had looked out the window before opening the door. I thought, *If I tell him my parents aren't here, he might barge his way into the house, but if I tell him my mom is expected home soon, maybe he will leave, knowing she will be home any minute.* I answered, "My mom will be home in a few minutes. Can you come back later?" It worked! He turned and left without saying a word but I thought it was odd that he didn't stop at any of the neighbors' houses. It was true; our mom was expected home from work very soon.

About thirty minutes later, our mom arrived, and we told her about the peculiar salesman who might be returning. She didn't seem concerned at all and told us she had to run to the store around the corner and would be right back. We watched from the living room window as our mom's car disappeared around the corner about four houses down. As soon as her car was out of sight, the salesman appeared from the same corner, as if he had been waiting for her to leave. He started walking toward our house at a fast pace, only this time, he was not carrying a vacuum. We screamed and locked the doors then ran to the back bedroom and hid under a desk. My sister started to cry. I told her to be quiet so he wouldn't know we were home. We waited in silence. My heart was beating so fast.

Suddenly, the doorbell rang. We gasped, and I put my hand over my mouth. He rang again, then began banging on the door with his fist. We were terrified! We heard the storm door creak open and the doorknob started rattling as he tried to open our front door. I prayed under my breath, "God, please help us!" The storm door slammed shut, and there was silence. We didn't know if he was gone or if he was going around to the back door. We were too afraid to come out because he might see us through the window. We stayed under the desk, afraid to move. A few minutes later, we were relieved to hear our mother's car pulling into the driveway. We hysterically told her about the man trying to get in. She called the police, and they came to ask questions and file a report.

When I cried out to God from under that desk, He rescued us. I'm so thankful I can call on Him whenever I am afraid, knowing He is always there. In Psalm 23, one of the most familiar and comforting passages in the Bible, David speaks of God as the Good Shepherd, leading and protecting His sheep. Who better to write about a shepherd than a shepherd himself? It says, "Yea, though I walk through the valley of the shadow of death, I will fear no evil: for thou art with me; thy rod and thy staff they comfort me." Without a shepherd, the sheep are easy targets for predators. What a beautiful allegory reminding us that we don't have to be afraid, knowing God is our Good Shepherd ready to protect us whenever we are in danger.

🎼 *Under His wings I am safely abiding,*
Tho the night deepens and tempests are wild;
Still I can trust Him—I know He will keep me,
He has redeemed me and I am His child.
"Under His Wings"

You are my hiding place; you will save me from trouble.
I sing aloud of your salvation, because you protect me.

PSALM 32:7 GNT

17

Spread Your Wings

*He tends his flock like a shepherd: He gathers the lambs
in his arms and carries them close to his heart;
he gently leads those that have young.*

ISAIAH 40:11

WHEN I BECAME A MOTHER and held that baby girl for the first time I instantaneously fell deeply in love. My love for her was so overwhelming I thought my heart would burst. But at the same time, I was struck with fear knowing I was responsible for another human being. I was only twenty years old, and I think it was the first time in my life I realized I couldn't rely on my mother because I had just become a mother myself. I was also surprised how quickly I transformed into a "mother bear" with an incredible instinct to do anything to protect my baby girl. Eighteen years later, when I became a grandmother, I had the same instinct to protect my grandchild as I did when my children were born. I saw my grandbaby as an extension of my child. Especially, Mariah and Josiah, whose mothers were living with me at the time of their birth. Let me be clear, I realize my grandchildren are not *my* responsibility. God gave them parents to nurture and protect them. What I am saying is that I would do anything to protect my grandchildren as I would my own child.

One of the most difficult aspects of being a grandparent is to step back when my impulse so strongly wants to step in.

For instance, when my grandson Jacob started kindergarten, he insisted on riding the big yellow bus his first day of school. I had concerns about him going on this venture without the watchful eye of a parent or grandparent. My irrational fear stemmed from my sister's experience when her firstborn got off the bus at the wrong stop—on his first day of kindergarten—in *San Diego*! I would have died a million deaths. I don't blame Deb for homeschooling after that traumatic incident!

I wasn't there for Jacob's first day of school, but when I later asked him, "Were you afraid to ride the bus home from school?" his eyes lit up with excitement and he gleamed, "No, it was awesome!" I still worried about him riding the bus with all those big kids until he proved he could take care of himself. It was still the first week of school and his other grandma was waiting to get him off the bus when she noticed a kid with a bloody nose. She asked the boy's mom, "What happened to him?" The boy pointed at Jacob and whimpered, "He punched me!" It wasn't exactly the best way to start off his first year of school, but it reassured me that Jacob could fend

for himself. When we asked Jacob why he had punched the boy he said, "We were just playing around, punching each other in the arm and the kid told me to punch him harder, so I did!" Jacob felt bad about what had happened and said he didn't mean to hurt him. He has a tender heart and would never purposely hurt anyone. It wasn't long before Jacob and that boy became best buddies.

If only we all could be so bold to spread our wings and fearlessly fly into the world. It's not easy to put our children and grandchildren into the hands of God. But if we remind ourselves that He is the Good Shepherd who loves and cares for His sheep, it's easier to relinquish our cares to Him as we send our children off with a prayer. When we train our children up in the Lord and pray with them each morning, they will develop a habit of turning to God for all of their needs.

Have I not commanded you? Be strong and courageous. Do not be afraid; do not be discouraged, for the LORD your God will be with you wherever you go. JOSHUA 1:9

18

Zombies

*So we can confidently say, "The Lord is my helper;
I will not fear; what can man do to me?"*

HEBREWS 13:6 ESV

FOR NINE YEARS we lived in a home near a cemetery. I called it our estate because it had almost two acres of land with a half-acre pond and it backed up to a cornfield, which gave us lots of privacy. I loved our backyard because it was like a wildlife refuge and sanctuary. We regularly spotted deer, pheasants, quail, wild turkey, coyotes, wolves, geese, ducks, snapping and painted turtles, bluebirds, owls, and "Buster" the groundhog, who lived near the pond. One evening, we witnessed a rare phenomenon as three great horned owls ran across the yard chasing locusts. We also enjoyed watching beautiful sunsets over the field every evening. I loved living there because it felt like being in the country. It was my oasis.

We had an Australian cattle dog (also known as a blue heeler) named Spur. He was bred to herd cattle, and when he was a puppy he liked to nip at our heels. We worked hard to let him know we were humans and it was unacceptable for him to bite our feet. That dog was tough enough to make a ton of beef obey him, but we reformed him into a domesticated housedog. He had a lot of energy, so the first thing I did after a long day at work was take him for a walk in the cemetery. He was strong and loved to be in charge. I wasn't sure if I was taking him for a walk or if it was the other way around.

After one particularly exhausting day at work, I decided to tether him out back and take a walk by myself, without him pulling me down the road. I headed out to the cemetery on my usual route, and as I approached the farthest road in the deepest area of the graveyard, I noticed a man standing beside his car. As I got closer, I noticed his car had an out-of-state license plate, and at that moment, my instinct was to turn around, but I didn't. He was alone, just standing there looking over the top of his car at me, and I reassured myself, *He's probably just visiting a grave*. But honestly, at that moment, I regretted leaving my cattle dog at home. As I got closer, he walked to the front of his car toward me, his sinister eyes locked with mine, and he inquired, "Aren't you afraid to be out here alone? There could be zombies or something out here." I tried to act nonchalant. I furrowed my brow, squinted my eyes, curled my lip, and snarled, "No—that's ridiculous; I don't believe in zombies," and kept right on walking past his car. It was a rusty old station wagon with faux-wood panel sides, and as I passed the back end—without turning my head—out of the corner of my eye I saw a bunch of pillows, blankets, and some rope. My heart picked up speed along with my pace, and once again, I regretted leaving Spur at home. I thought, *If I scream, Spur might hear me, break free of his chain, and run to my rescue.* I walked faster and turned to see if the man was following me; he wasn't, but he was still watching from his car. I prayed for God to protect me and walked a little farther before turning around again and thankfully, he was gone.

I thanked God for protecting me and always being there to comfort me when I need Him. Deuteronomy 31:6 says, "Be strong and courageous; do not be afraid or terrified because of them, for the Lord your God goes with you; he will never leave you nor forsake you." I know it was Him who gave me the confidence not to run or show fear, which might have caused a different outcome. I will never underestimate the power of the Holy Spirit, who lives in me and manifests Himself in ways I'm not even aware.

He will cover you with his feathers,
and under his wings you will find refuge.
PSALM 91:4

19

A Cup of Tea

*They share freely and give generously to those in
need. Their good deeds will be remembered forever.
They will have influence and honor.*

PSALM 112:9 NLT

I SAT IN MY FAVORITE BLUE CHAIR sipping Earl Grey tea as I watched the yellow flames in the fireplace dance back and forth like a well-rehearsed tango. The wood crackled and popped as sparks from the glowing embers floated up the chimney. I watched as a ladybug flew erratically, tapping against the dome light, and would probably end up dead inside like the other two. I took another sip of my tea, and memories of my great aunt Dorothy Kinne came flooding back to me because she is the one who introduced me to afternoon tea. Sadly, she passed away in the year 2000 at the age of ninety-five, but she had lived a very full life. She was like a grandmother to me, and I cherish the relationship we developed over the last decade of her life.

When she was eighty years old, I began going to her home every other weekend to clean, buy groceries, and do her laundry. After I finished cleaning, she would invite me to sit at her dining room table for a cup of tea and an oatmeal raisin cookie. I treasured this time with her, as I listened to stories of her childhood, the struggles of living through the Great Depression and how her life had changed over the years. I can't imagine the burden her husband must have felt, standing on a corner selling apples, wondering where they would get their next meal. But nothing compared to the pain of losing her two-year-old daughter, who died from meningitis because at that time there was no treatment. I remember Aunt Dorothy telling me, "My daughter died one year before penicillin was discovered. It was one year too late for her." Oh, how she missed her daughter! She confessed that she never got over the grief of losing a child. She also had two sons, whom she adored, but the loss of her only daughter devastated her.

    Aunt Dorothy taught me many things about my heritage. For instance, her mother, my great-grandmother, was a dressmaker. In the 1900's dresses required a substantial amount of material. When her customers discarded an old dress, she would use the material to make dresses for her three daughters. She passed that skill down to Dorothy, who lovingly handmade Christmas stockings for my children from her old clothing. They were intricately designed from burgundy fabric with an olive-green cuff. She fashioned a beige pocket on the front and trimmed it with rickrack. Using red velvet she

appliqued a cat on one and a bear on the other as if to peek out of the pockets. She hand embroidered their faces with eyes, nose, ears, and whiskers, then for the finishing touch, she added a tiny red satin bow and placed it on their necks. Every Christmas when I hang those prized possessions on my mantel I feel the love and care she put into those treasured gifts.

Dorothy had a great impact on my life. I realized how sweet life could be when spent with someone you love. It all started with a cup of tea, sitting at her dining room table. I learned the importance of sharing stories and life with those you love, because you never know the impact it will have on somebody's life. Cherished memories are for a lifetime.

She makes linen garments and sells them; she delivers sashes to the merchant. Strength and dignity are her clothing, and she laughs at the time to come. She opens her mouth with wisdom, and the teaching of kindness is on her tongue.

PROVERBS 31:24-26 ESV

20
Worry Warrior

*Anxiety in the heart of man causes depression,
but a good word makes it glad.*

PROVERBS 12:25 NKJV

I THOUGHT I WAS GOING TO DIE if I got on the ship. My husband and I were planning a trip to celebrate our twenty-fifth anniversary. We would fly to Miami, get on a ship, and cruise around the Caribbean Sea. I had gotten our Last Will and Testament notarized just in case, by some fluke, the plane crashed or the ship sank, leaving my children as orphans. I have an unhealthy fear of water to begin with, so the thought of being on a ship in the middle of the ocean miles away from land was propelling me into a panic. I had seen *Titanic*, and I thought to myself, *If it happened once, it could happen again.* Never mind, we wouldn't be anywhere near icebergs—if the ship sank, I would be the cause; just like Jonah, I would be the reason for trouble at sea.

My son, John, was listening to my ridiculous, irrational concerns. He turned to me and said something that taught me an important lesson. With all of his twenty-three years of wisdom, he said, "Mom, when it's your time to go you will go, whether you're on a plane, on a ship, or sitting in that chair!" I immediately felt convicted, realizing my son had more faith than his worried, fearful mother. He was right. God has a plan for every one of us, and nothing we do in our own scheme of things will change our God-ordained time to die.

Worry seems to be a common problem for many people, even though it won't change the outcome or prevent bad things from happening. It's futile. All it does is hurt our health by causing stress, increasing blood pressure, lowering immunity, and turning our joy into depression. Worry happens when we fail to have faith that God is in control of our lives. Fear is the opposite of faith. God knew we would struggle with fear because the most common command in the Bible is "Fear not." Fear is a complicated emotion. It can repel us from danger, motivate us to study harder, or incarcerate us, preventing us from being able to enjoy life.

I confess that I have a tendency to worry about everything, and the older I get, the more fearful I become as I worry something bad will happen to my children or grandchildren. It was starting to consume me to the point my kids were telling me, "Mom, you worry too much." Even my five-year-old grandson would say, "Grammy, stop worrying. I'm fine!" Sometimes I would check Facebook to see what my kids were up to, and when I saw them having loads of fun, I realized my fears were completely unfounded. I have learned to pray instead of worry, but it's an ongoing struggle. Once I turn it over to God, I am not consumed by it anymore.

Usually, the very thing we worry about never happens, so it's a waste of time that could be spent having fun ourselves. Life throws enough stress at us; we don't need to create figments of our imagination to compound it! When we learn to relinquish our fears to God, our worry will be replaced with peace and joy. Don't let worry rob you from happiness. Pray about it, then go about your day knowing God has everything under control.

Therefore do not worry about tomorrow,
for tomorrow will worry about its own things.
Sufficient for the day is its own trouble.
MATTHEW 6:34 NKJV

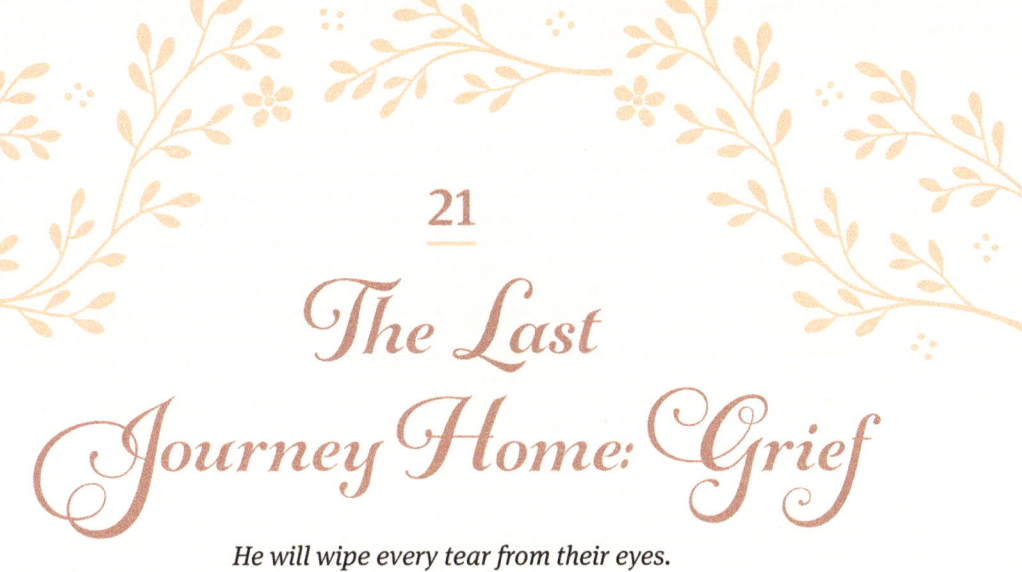

21
The Last Journey Home: Grief

He will wipe every tear from their eyes.
There will be no more death or mourning or crying
or pain, for the old order of things has passed away.

REVELATION 21:4

THE SOFT VIBRATIONS from my phone quietly woke me up at three in the morning. It was my turn to give Mom her medication. I got up from my air mattress in the adjacent room where I had been trying to sleep since she was brought home on hospice. I felt guilty sleeping at all, but I knew I wouldn't be good to anyone if I didn't at least try. Every time I roused, I would lift my head from the bed to study her breathing, or I would get up to feel her skin, assessing whether she was too warm or not warm enough, and I'd swab her tongue with a lemon stick to soothe her dry mouth. She couldn't tell me what she needed because she hadn't spoken a word or opened her eyes in the past four days. I felt out of my realm as a nurse because my job was to save lives, not care for the dying. It felt surreal, but it also was an honor to keep vigil for the mother who so many times had done the same for me.

My sister Deb and her husband were sleeping in the guest room, so I tried to be quiet and not wake them, since one of them had taken the last shift. I went into the kitchen and carefully measured the liquid medication, drawing it up in a syringe. I walked over to Mom's hospital bed, gently took her hand in mine, and watched her take deep, regular breaths. I whispered, "Hi, Mom, it's Judy. I'm going to give you some medicine to make you more comfortable." I slowly administered the pain-relieving drug under her tongue, a little at a time, then sat in the chair next to her bed where each of my siblings, my father, and I had been taking turns comforting her over the past ten days. As I sat with her hand in mine, I laid my head on the bed and prayed for her comfort and peace, wondering how much longer she would have to suffer on this final journey home. The previous few days, my father, my siblings, our spouses, and I had stood at her bedside, singing hymns, praying, and reading Scripture to the woman who had lovingly cared for us as a true servant of Christ. We knew she would soon be in a place with no more pain, no more tears, and no more suffering.

On November 7, 2017, my loving mother entered the presence of the Lord—it was God's time to call her home. The moment she died, my father embraced me and spoke these words into my ear: "But as it is written, what no eye hath seen, nor ear heard, nor heart of man imagined, what God has prepared for those who love him—in the twinkling of an eye, she was there!" I can't think of anything more comforting than to hear my father speaking the Word of God at the same moment my mother was meeting Him face to face. As I was being held in my father's arms, the Father in heaven was embracing my mother. I envisioned her standing before the Lord with her glorified body, hearing the words, "Well done, good and faithful servant!" She was finally home!

It hurts when we lose someone we love, but those who believe can have hope of one day being reunited in heaven. First Thessalonians 4:13 tells us we are not to grieve as those who have no hope. We knew our mother was rejoicing in the presence of the Lord because of her faith in Christ's death on the cross. Jesus sacrificed His life so we could be with Him forever and never have to say good-bye again. His death paid the penalty for our sins and opened the gates of heaven for those who believe and trust Him as their Savior. That is our hope—to one day see Him face to face—and to be reunited with those who are already there.

But, as it is written, "What no eye has seen,
nor ear heard, nor the heart of man imagined,
what God has prepared for those who love him."
1 CORINTHIANS 2:9 ESV

22

The Uninvited House Guest

For since the creation of the world God's invisible qualities—his eternal power and divine nature—have been clearly seen. ROMANS 1:20

I LET OUT A BLOOD-CURDLING SCREAM when it caught my eye. It was a dark and stormy night when I was letting my dog outside to do his business. I opened the door, trying not to get wet from the pouring rain, as I watched my Australian cattle dog run out into the dark. As I stood holding the door open, I felt something scratch across the tops of my feet. My first thought was, *Why did the dog run back into the house? I just let him out.* I looked down, and out of the corner of my eye I saw a large moving object in my family room. I turned my head with a jerk and felt the blood leaving my face. A huge possum was scurrying across the floor, his mangy body rolling side to side with each step, while his long wiry tail creepily bobbed up and down with each step. I screamed so loudly that the windows shook!

Mike was upstairs when he heard it. He sprang from his chair and jumped down five steps at a time, his heart racing from the adrenaline, as he prepared to witness some horrific scene from a horror movie. "Look, over there!" I shrieked, pointing at the huge, rat-like beast with black beady eyes hissing at us. By now our two preteen girls were standing on the stairs, peering from a safe distance to see what all the commotion was about. Mike turned to Abby and demanded, "Go to the garage and bring me a shovel!" He thought if he could just nudge the critter into the dog's crate using a shovel, he could then carry it outside. Abigail returned, only she didn't have a shovel. She blurted out, "I couldn't find the shovel, so I grabbed this." She held up a swiveling Swiffer dust mop.

Mike took the Swiffer and held it against the possum's neck, but it kept swiveling, so he couldn't get good leverage. The dog had returned from doing his business and was barking uncontrollably, which only made matters worse. Mike continued to coax the 'possum into the crate using the Swiffer, and after what seemed like an eternity, he succeeded in getting the mangy rodent into the cage and out of the house. This scene became known as the "Swiffer incident," and we laugh every time we retell the story.

That marsupial was so ugly, and yet at the same time it seemed to have a smile on its face. God has a good sense of humor, creating such a despicable

and peculiar animal. It definitely gave our family a good laugh and the memory will be embedded in our minds forever.

I think all of God's creatures are a form of entertainment. I love to sit and watch the birds at my feeder, and I get excited when a fox or deer run through my yard. Every spring I look forward to the mallards that fly in to eat some cracked corn and make their nest. When the grandchildren visit, they like to walk down to the lake searching for blue heron, geese, ducks, turtles, carp, and a very busy muskrat. It's like going on a treasure hunt to see what unexpected creature will bring us joy. There is something special about seeing animals in nature. They are God's gifts to us.

Ask the animals, and they will teach you, or the birds in the sky, and they will tell you; or speak to the earth, and it will teach you, or let the fish in the sea inform you. Which of all these does not know that the hand of the Lord has done this? In his hand is the life of every creature and the breath of all mankind. JOB 12:7-10

23

Fixer Upper

*Therefore, if anyone is in Christ, he is a new creation.
The old has passed away; behold, the new has come.*

2 CORINTHIANS 5:17 ESV

I WOULDN'T DESCRIBE IT as my dream home when I first saw it, but I had a vision that it could become something beautiful. When we first drove up to the house, the front lawn was so tall it looked more like a field of prairie grass. My husband, Mike, and I knew it would be a fixer upper. We parked in the street and walked up the horseshoe driveway that desperately needed repairing. I glanced at the flowerbeds, which were overgrown with weeds. The realtor pointed to them and declared, "There are some really nice flowers in there."

We entered the front door and cringed when we saw the green wool carpet. We surmised it could possibly be original to the house, which was built in 1959, so it only dated back a mere forty years. The family room could be described somewhere between hideous and repugnant, with its dark wood paneling and burnt sienna plaid carpet, but we were impressed with the heated floor that would be a bonus during the winter. We scratched our heads as we pondered why there was a woodburning stove peculiarly placed in front of a beautiful stone fireplace. As odd and distasteful as it was, I saw past all the muck in that room and envisioned our family gathering there for holidays, birthdays, and movie nights. We ventured upstairs to the bathroom, which was equally out of date with its matching pink sink, pink toilet, and pink tub. But what really raised my eyebrows was the antiquated boomerang pattern that was printed on the formica vanity top. We made our way out the back door into the sea of tall grass, and it took our breath away. The real estate agent explained, "This property has nearly two acres of land, including the half-acre, spring-fed pond." Sold! We saw the potential of that ramshackle house and didn't hesitate to make an offer. As we waited for the owners to respond to our bid, I imagined myself sitting on the deck, drinking some tea, watching the sun set over the horizon. It was going to be my oasis—and it was.

    We closed the deal on Mother's Day, which seemed appropriate since it was my mother who spotted the house and suggested we check it out. On the day we signed a contract, the front yard was being dug up to put in a new water line, and a tractor was baling the waist-high grass out back. We were so excited to start renovating our fixer upper. On our first day of possession, I eagerly began cleaning the kitchen. I went over to the stove top and was about to start wiping it down when a mouse poked its head up through one of the burners. We replaced the old carpet and gave each room a fresh coat of paint. We removed the sooty wood-burning stove and

repaired the hole in the wall, where it had hooked up to the chimney. Over the years, we gave life to that dilapidated house and transformed it into our beautiful home. We will fondly remember the chorus of frogs in our pond every spring, late-night bonfires under the shooting stars, and lying in bed listening to the squirrel scratching inside the wall after getting in through a hole in the soffit. Renovating that house was a labor of love, rewarded by cherished memories tucked away as heirlooms of our past.

That old house needed a lot of fixing up, just as our lives constantly need repairs too. When we put our trust in Christ, we become a new person. He transforms us into something new and beautiful. We will constantly have battles between the old nature and the new. Romans 7:19 says, For I do not do the good I want to do, but the evil I do not want to do—this I keep on doing. But we are God's workmanship, and He will continue preparing us for the day of redemption, when we will receive our new, glorified bodies."

And I am sure of this, that he who began a good work in you, will bring it to completion at the day of Jesus Christ.
PHILIPPIANS 1:6 ESV

24
Christmas at the White House

Every good and perfect gift is from above.
JAMES 1:17

IN DECEMBER OF 2017, one of my all-time dreams came true. It all started on December 4, 2017, when I received a call from US Congressman Darin LaHood's office: "Hello, we received your request for tickets to tour the White House. I'm sorry this is such late notice, but we have tickets for you to tour this Thursday, December 7th."

I was ecstatic because for many years my favorite show has been *Christmas at the White House*, which airs on HGTV. It's like the Super Bowl for me; I look forward to it every year. So, naturally, I was floating on air. My husband and I took time off from our jobs, booked a hotel, and had one day to prepare for the eleven-hour drive to Washington, DC.

On the morning of December 7th, Congressman LaHood met us at the gate and escorted us past multiple safety checks, armed guards, and metal detectors. We entered through the East Wing, stopping at the East landing to admire the Gold Star Family tree, which pays homage to the armed forces and their families. Decorated in red, white, and blue, the tree also exhibits gold ornaments that bear names of heroes who made the ultimate sacrifice for our country. We strolled through the East Colonnade lined with painted white tree branches covered in white lights and proceeded to the East Garden Room where holiday cards from previous presidents were on display in glass shadow boxes. The Vermeil Room, known as the First Lady's sitting room, was decorated in classy gold accents, which seemed appropriate next to the sophisticated portrait of Jacqueline Kennedy.

The next stop was the library. In the middle of the room, green books formed the likeness of a tree while a garland made of shiny green balls and bright red bows modestly dressed the mantel. The China Room was resplendent with its eight-foot portrait of Dolly Madison. The magnificent centerpiece was a gilded bronze plateau set with mirrors, ordered by James Monroe in 1817. The room had gilded urns down the center filled with bright red roses and fresh green sprigs. The table was set with Ronald Reagan china, gold utensils, and embossed cloth napkins, ready for a grand holiday dinner. We climbed the back staircase to the largest room in the house, the East Room, which hosts dozens of holiday parties every year. Lush garlands cascaded onto the floor from all four mantels, and the elaborate eighteenth-century crèche, with a crowned baby Jesus, was on display for its fiftieth year.

History came alive in the famous Green Room, where Thomas Jefferson hosted state dinners. The garland draped over the mantel was filled with gold-framed silhouettes of presidents. The Red Room, named for the red

tapestry-covered walls, was my favorite. The theme for this room was treats and candy, decorated with glass containers filled with red and white peppermint treats. The tree was wrapped in red and white bows, and sugar cookies were tied to the tree with red ribbons. The finale of our tour concluded in the Grand Foyer, which had been transformed into a winter wonderland. The fifty plus trees were covered in white lights, crystal nutcrackers, shimmering icicles, and soft, cottony snow dusted the branches, creating a magical scene.

Touring the White House was one of the most incredible experiences of my life, but it will pale in comparison to the place God is preparing in heaven. The Book of Revelation describes the New Jerusalem as a city of pure gold, clear as crystal with the glory of the Lord shining so bright that there will be no need of a sun or moon. When I decorate my home with sparkly chandeliers and shiny objects, it's a reflection of my yearning for what God is preparing for me in heaven, but nothing on this earth will even compare to what God is preparing for those who love Him.

I saw the Holy City, the New Jerusalem, coming down out of heaven from God, prepared as a bride beautifully dressed for her husband.

REVELATION 21:2

25
Epiphany in the Garden

Ponder the path of your feet;
then all your ways will be sure.

PROVERBS 4:26 ESV

I INHALED THE SWEET FRAGRANCE of cherry blossoms as we walked through the gate. My husband and I were at the Missouri Botanical Gardens, one of the most beautiful places I had ever seen. The cadence of harmonious colors drew us in as we left our busy lives at the door and entered a sanctuary full of God's creation. The winding paths led us by the azalea-covered hills, past the enchanting beds of tulips, daffodils, and fragrant hyacinth, into the picturesque Japanese Garden. Weeping willows billowed over the pond where large koi congregated, swimming over and under each other near the water's edge. Amethyst wisteria hung like succulent grapes from an arbor, not unlike a Claude Monet painting. I imagined I had entered the Garden of Eden, wondering how Adam and Eve must have felt in the beginning of time.

Mike and I were there on our thirty-fifth anniversary, and he was pushing me in a wheelchair. Five years earlier, a torn meniscus and arthroscopic surgery had damaged my knee, and I needed a knee replacement. I was only fifty-four years old, so I kept putting it off because I had observed the ghastly operation when I worked in the OR and, honestly, it terrified me. Mike pushed me down the walkways, over a bridge, and past elderly visitors who were able to walk better than me. It was humiliating to be sitting in a wheelchair at such a young age, and I thought to myself, *This is ridiculous*! Right then and there I decided I would go ahead with the operation. Two months later, I had a total knee replacement and got my mobility and my life back. Unfortunately, since I had delayed the surgery for so long, there was a lot of damage, which made the operation and rehabilitation much more complicated. But after months of physical therapy, I fully recovered, and my mobility returned to normal. I am so thankful to be able to walk again, and not a day goes by that I take it for granted.

My life was not a bed of roses that day at the botanical gardens. My knee pain was so horrific I couldn't even walk. How many times do our lives get messy from going off the path, making a bad decision, and dabbling in sin when we know we shouldn't? Those poor choices wreak havoc on our lives, and afterward we must pay the consequences. I should have had the knee surgery long before the pain got that severe. Because I had waited so long to have my knee replacement, the recovery time took longer than

usual. It's the same way with sin. When we continue to live outside God's principles, we get deeper into trouble and it is much more difficult to get our lives back on track. So much damage has been done that it won't be easy to fix. It's like taking a wrong turn on the interstate and driving for miles in the wrong direction. The farther we travel away from our destination, the longer it will take to get back on track. Sin might be fun for a season, but it sows destruction, to us and to those we love. Sin damages relationships and ruins reputations but, more importantly, it disrupts our fellowship with God. He doesn't want us to live a life of turmoil, depression, and heartache. He loves us, but He also has rules to be followed; otherwise, we will experience trouble. Your actions will have repercussions. You cannot escape them. If you sow destruction, you reap destruction; but if you sow good behavior, you will reap a harvest.

*Do not be deceived: God is not mocked,
for whatever one sows, that will he also reap.*

GALATIANS 6:7 ESV

26

He Knows My Name

*I am the good shepherd.
I know my own and my own know me.*

JOHN 10:14 ESV

THE YEAR WAS 1958 when my parents were renting an old farmhouse complete with a horse, dog, dairy cow, and some pigs. One cold winter morning, my dad went out to feed the animals and noticed a little piglet lying on the ground away from the warmth of its mother. He put her inside his coat and took her inside the house. When he tried to feed her with a nipple, she was too weak to suck, so he squeezed milk into her mouth one drop at a time. He placed her in a box lined with a soft blanket and set it next to the heater. In a matter of minutes, the piglet perked right up, and my dad knew she would be all right. Mom named the piglet Petunia and kept her inside as a pet, nursing her along for a couple of weeks until she was strong enough to return to the harsh elements outside. The day arrived when she was ready to return to her mother, so Dad took her out to the hog pen and placed her on the ground. She ran over to the other pigs, and surprisingly, they accepted her back as if she was never gone.

My parents moved away from the farm when Petunia was eight months old. Sometime later they returned to the farm, and my mom wondered if her pet pig would recognize her name. She went over to the fence and called, "Petunia!" Out from the herd, a pig came running toward her, squealing and grunting. Mom knew it was Petunia because when Dad rescued her, part of her tail had broken off from frostbite.

Just like Petunia never forgot her name, God never forgets ours. He knew us and loved us before we were born. Whoever believes in Him will have his or her name written down in the Book of Life, and when we get to heaven, He will know us. But for those who reject Him and don't believe in Him, He will say, "I never knew you," and they will spend eternity in hell, forever separated from God. It's our decision to make. He sends out the invitations, but unless we accept it, our names won't be on the guest list. God doesn't wish that any should perish, but He lets us choose to believe in Him or not. John 3:16 says, "For God so loved the world that he gave his one and only Son, that whoever believes in him shall not perish but have eternal life."

When Mary was newly pregnant with Jesus, she visited her cousin, Elizabeth, who was pregnant with John the Baptist. As soon as Mary greeted her, the baby in Elizabeth's womb jumped, and Elizabeth was filled with the Holy Spirit and said, "Blessed are you among women, and blessed is

the child you will bear! But why am I so favored, that the mother of my Lord should come to me? As soon as the sound of your greeting reached my ears, the baby in my womb leaped for joy. Blessed is she who has believed that the Lord would fulfill his promises to her!" (Luke 1:42–45).

Elizabeth referred to Mary as "the mother of my Lord," and John, who was only six months into development, leaped in excitement. Before a child is born, God knows his or her name and has a plan for their life: "Before I formed you in the womb, I knew you, and before you were born I consecrated you" (Jeremiah 1:5 ESV).

When you first meet someone, before you know their name they are a stranger, but once you are introduced and you get acquainted, then you *know* them. God *knows* us. He doesn't need any introductions. He calls us by name. I am His, and He is mine.

Fear not, for I have redeemed you;
I have called you by name, you are mine.

ISAIAH 43:1 ESV

27
God's Angels

When God's people are in need, be ready to help them.
Always be eager to practice hospitality.

ROMANS 12:13 NLT

I WAS SHOPPING in a Christian bookstore when I saw a book I thought would be perfect for my friend who was going through a divorce. I felt led to buy it, and I took it right over to her house. I sensed an urgency to go straight there from the store. When I arrived, my friend said she had been crying uncontrollably, for hours, praying for help. When she saw me, she broke down and said, "You are my angel; I prayed for an angel and you were sent to me!" A week later, she said she had read the entire book in one sitting, and it was exactly what she needed. She told me it really encouraged her, to know that I cared and was praying for her.

The Lord spoke to me in another situation and prompted me to visit my mother-in-law, who had been in ICU for weeks with little hope of recovering. Her sister had been at the hospital for hours, comforting my father-in-law. They needed a distraction, so they decided to head for the cafeteria. While they waited for the elevator, she declared, "When those elevator doors open, an angel will be there." When the doors opened, I was standing in the elevator. She looked surprised when she saw me and gasped, putting her hand on her chest. Then she placed her hands on my shoulders, looked me in the eye and said, "Judy, you are my angel. I prayed for an angel, and here you are!" How amazing is God that He uses us to be His hands and feet? God used *me* to comfort her when she needed encouragement.

It reminds me of a story in Matthew 25, where Jesus is telling a parable about being rewarded with the kingdom of God. He says: "'For I was hungry and you gave me food, I was thirsty and you gave me drink, I was a stranger and you welcomed me, I was naked and you clothed me, I was sick and you visited me, I was in prison and you came to me.' Then the righteous will answer him, saying, 'Lord, when did we see you hungry and feed you, or thirsty and give you drink? And when did we see you sick or in prison and visit you?' And the King will answer them, 'Truly, I say to you, as you did it to one of the least of these my brothers, you did it to me'" (vv. 35–40 ESV).

Have you ever felt led to contact someone, send a card, pay a visit, or deliver a meal, and it turned out to be exactly what that person needed? God uses us to meet the needs of hurting people in a world filled with pain and suffering. We are His hands, His voice, and His feet to those who need encouragement.

Therefore, my beloved brothers, be steadfast, immovable, always abounding in the work of the Lord, knowing that in the Lord your labor is not in vain.

1 CORINTHIANS 15:58 ESV

28
Rekindle the Flame

Do nothing out of selfish ambition or vain conceit.
Rather, in humility value others above yourselves.

PHILIPPIANS 2:3

IT BROKE MY HEART to think my husband and I had drifted apart, and after Mike went upstairs to bed, I sat alone in the living room wondering how this could have happened. It made no sense because our last child had fledged from the nest, leaving us with more time to connect on a deeper level. I guess I wouldn't say our marriage was in trouble, but it wasn't filled with the love and excitement of our younger days.

Let me start by saying I love my husband with all my heart. He is the kindest, gentlest man I have ever met. He would do anything to make me happy to a fault, and he serves me in ways I don't deserve. In some ways, I would say I won the jackpot when it comes to a man devoted to his wife. So why did our marriage feel stagnant? Mike has always been a good provider. He doesn't drink alcohol or go on weeklong fishing trips with the guys, like some of his friends. He likes being at home watching movies or reading, and I have never had to worry about him having an affair—that I am sure. I'm not saying he is perfect; there are plenty of days when I want to drive off in my Camaro to take a breather. But love sees past the other's faults and focuses on the good in others. I'm saying, marriage is not built on easy street for anybody, it takes a lot of work. It just seemed like our interests had changed over the years, and we started going in different directions. I think the freedom from our empty nest had spurned a desire to pursue completely different paths, and it worried me.

The next morning, we had a heart-to-heart talk where I expressed my perception that a change had taken place in our relationship. We agreed to spend more time in God's Word because when we fill ourselves up with the love of God, we stop waiting to be served and look for ways to serve others, which can apply to all relationships. When we focus on ourselves, we demand that our own needs be met rather than being aware of the other person's needs. We try to blame each other for our lack of fulfillment, when the emptiness we feel is our selfishness.

Mike and I came up with a plan: to address any problems early on *before* a molehill becomes a mountain and the slightest trigger causes a volcanic eruption of angry, hurtful words that have been smoldering beneath the surface. We made a commitment to have date night at least once a week with electronic devices put away so our focus can be on each other. We came up with a list of things we love doing together, such as: going on a picnic in the park, taking a walk holding hands, or going ballroom dancing with the senior citizens because it makes us feel young again. Sometimes we even add a little romance by having a candlelight dinner at home. Romance doesn't have to cost a penny, and it's a great way to rekindle a fire that needs to be stoked. If the love in your marriage isn't what it used to be, have a talk, make a plan, be creative, and start dating again.

Be devoted to one another in love.
Honor one another above yourselves.
ROMANS 12:10

29
Trust Like Noah, Not Jonah

*LORD, I know that people's lives are not their own;
it is not for them to direct their steps.*

JEREMIAH 10:23

FIVE YEARS INTO OUR MARRIAGE my husband announced, "I'm quitting my job and going to college." I'm sure he could feel the daggers being thrown at him from my eyes. He went on to explain, "I need to get a college degree. This printing job is a dead end, and I want to be able to provide for my family. We will live in married housing. I'll get a part-time job and take out student loans for the rest of our expenses so you will still be able to stay home with the kids."

Our children were ages three and four at the time, and even though Mike felt God was telling him to go, I was skeptical. He had more faith than I did. He wasn't asking me—he was telling me as the leader of the family, so I knew I had to follow. Part of me thought it sounded like an adventure because we had lived in the same small town our entire lives, but truthfully, I was terrified. I knew I had to trust God to take care of us. If God was telling my husband to go to college, I was not going to stand in the way.

For the next three years, he spent every waking moment studying, working, and going to school, burning the midnight oil. I made friends with our neighbors, which made my life easier since I felt like a single parent. Mike had little free time, but we made it work. We lived in a tiny apartment with paper-thin walls and the children next door were just as loud as ours; so Mike spent a lot of time studying at the library. There were days I would plead with him, "Please don't go. Study at home—I miss you!" but the kids were too loud and it distracted him, so he had to leave. I remember one hot summer day when Mike was away studying, the kids and I were filling up water balloons, and the handle on the spigot fell off with the water on full blast. I couldn't get the handle back on, and the water kept gushing, creating quite a puddle. Elizabeth was five at the time. She ran sobbing into the house and stood peering out the window, with a look of terror on her face. Finally, one of the neighbors came to my rescue and was able to turn it off with some pliers. I went inside to console my distraught daughter and asked why she was crying. She sobbed, "I thought the earth was going to be flooded again!" I reassured her that God promised never to flood the earth again, and the rainbow is a sign of His promise. I had never thought of Noah's ark as a scary story, but to a small child who takes things so literally, I guess it could be frightening.

After three long arduous years, Mike's hard work and determination rewarded him. He graduated with the highest distinction and honorary title of *summa cum laude* with a perfect 4.0 GPA. He got a great-paying job right out of college, and our lives were changed completely. It wasn't easy

for either one of us, but looking back, those three short years were nothing compared to the many years of financial stability it gave our future. When God calls—go—because His ways are higher than ours and He knows what's best for us.

I think about Jonah, who didn't want to go to Nineveh. He ended up spending three days in the belly of a fish, which finally got his attention to go where God was sending him. I had to trust God to provide for us those three years while Mike worked part-time. We had some short weeks and ate pancakes for dinner a few nights in a row, but we never went hungry, and the bills were always paid on time. Just as Noah had to trust God when he was asked to build the ark, we had to trust Him too. God flooded the earth, because people were living sinful lives, and only Noah was found to be righteous, so his family was spared. Even though God promised to never flood the earth again, Noah's and Jonah's stories should still strike fear in those who choose to go their own way rather than listen to God. Mike heard God leading him to go to college and our lives were blessed beyond measure.

Trust in the Lord with all your heart; do not depend on your own understanding, Seek his will in all you do, and he will show you which path to take.

PROVERBS 3:5–6 NLT

30
Forgive & Forget

*Be kind and compassionate to one another,
forgiving each other, just as in Christ God forgave you.*

EPHESIANS 4:32

IT IS DIFFICULT TO FORGIVE SOMEONE who has hurt you deeply. Whenever I think I can't forgive someone, I remind myself that Christ bore my sin and forgave me for every horrible thing I've ever done, so I have no right *not* to forgive someone. Probably the hardest person to forgive is myself—I beat myself up over and over as I replay an offense or situation I should have handled differently. The wound festers, but when I relinquish and forgive, the wound begins to heal and I can move on.

It's so easy to get stuck in the past, ruminating about something that can't be fixed or changed. This prevents us from moving forward; we can't go back and change the past. Dwelling on past sins or failures won't change the future, so let go of whatever is weighing you down, and free yourself with forgiveness. When we obsess over an offense or hurtful comment, it punishes us, not the offender. It's like fighting against a riptide. You will become exhausted and defeated unless you stop struggling and float along until it releases you. You must stop dwelling on your past to be free, so you can safely make it to the shore.

When inmates are released from prison after serving their time, they are free. If we harbor bad feelings about something, it keeps us locked up, and we can't enjoy life because we are dragging the ball and chain around with us. To move forward, the ruminating has to end. I'm not saying you need to invite the one who has offended you over for dinner, but rather, choose to focus on today, right now, starting with this moment. It may take a lot of training to control your thinking by redirecting it and choosing not to dwell on the offense. Put those negative thoughts on the shelf—they are there, and no one denies that, but walk away and leave them behind. Live each day as a new beginning so you can experience joy. God wants you to enjoy life and to be happy.

When God forgives us, He forgets, and as far as the east is from the west, it is gone (Psalm 103:12)! Matthew 6:14 says that if we forgive, then the Father will forgive us. Verse 15 continues: If we don't forgive, He won't forgive us. Your life will be miserable until you forgive and release the pain that is keeping you hostage.

When Christ was carrying the heavy cross to Golgotha, He was spat on, beaten, and called names by the very people He created, the people He

came to save, the people He was about to rescue from their sins by dying in their place so they could live. Those people didn't believe He was the Son of God. I can't imagine how heartrending that must have been for Him. The crowd mocked Him saying, "If you are King of the Jews, save yourself!" But He didn't save Himself because He loved us enough to die in our place so we could spend eternity with Him. While Christ was in the midst of dying one of the most horrific deaths, He said, "Father, forgive them, for they know not what they are doing" (Luke 23:34 ESV). He knew it had to be done, and when He completed His mission, He said, "It is finished." Then He gave up His spirit and breathed His last breath. Let Christ's example of forgiveness be the start of a new day as you forgive and move on to a life filled with joy and peace. Don't be caught in the riptide, it's time to be free.

And when you stand praying, if you hold anything against anyone, forgive them, so that your Father in heaven may forgive you your sins.

MARK 11:25

31

The Escape

Yes, my soul, finds rest in God;
my hope comes from him.

PSALM 62:5

MY HUSBAND, Mike, and I felt we should get away for a little while. Our daughter's family of eight moved in with us when the house they were expecting to move into was not ready, then one week later, Mike's father unexpectedly passed away. Mike had been given power of attorney for his dad four years before and now he was handling his father's estate. Our lives had been very hectic and it felt like we were caught in a whirlwind.

We decided to take a short trip to the French Lick Resort in Indiana to escape and enjoy some relaxation. Once we checked into our room Mike wanted to rest, so I did some exploring of the beautiful hotel, built in 1845. I found a quiet comfy spot in the mezzanine where my mind was put to rest. As I listened to Frank Sinatra playing over the speakers, I admired the gold-plated corbels, marble pillars, crystal chandeliers, and hand-painted scenes of angels on the ceiling. The walls were filled with photos of famous people who had been guests at the very glamorous hotel. I felt like a queen sitting in a palace. Only a cup of Earl Grey tea would have made it more complete.

When the sun began to set, giving some relief from the heat, we ventured onto the grand front porch where rows of rocking chairs overlooked the beautiful gardens. We sat in the light breeze of the ceiling fans where wealthy and prominent society members once gathered in the early 1900s. After a bit, we strolled next door to the West Baden Springs Hotel, built in 1855. It was once listed as the eighth wonder of the world because of its natural springs, but it smelled more like rotten eggs than a therapeutic spa. Apparently, the mineral springs are not very hot anymore.

We entered the hotel and our breath was taken away by the impressive two-hundred-foot-diameter atrium. Guest suites with balconies opened to a four-story-high dome overlooking the restaurant where we shared a romantic dinner while listening to a Beethoven symphony being played on the grand piano. The ambiance was like stepping back in time to a world of high society and glamor.

The French Lick was a perfect destination for some much-needed R&R. It felt good to turn off our cell phones and be free from the distractions of social media. Years ago, you could go for a walk and take a vacation without worrying about an interrupting text or phone call. It really helped us reconnect by getting away from our daily routines and responsibilities for some much needed rejuvenation.

Even Christ had to escape the crowds and find time to be alone and pray. He went away to prepare for His ministries. He went away to deal with grief. He went away after teaching the crowds, and He went away to prepare for His death. It's no wonder spending time away from our busy lives helps restore us as it did for Christ.

Oh, that I had the wings of a dove!
I would fly away and be at rest.
PSALM 55:6

32
Mirror, Mirror

Therefore we do not lose heart.
Though outwardly we are wasting away,
yet inwardly we are being renewed day by day.

2 CORINTHIANS 4:16

MIRROR, MIRROR, what do you see? *I see a middle-aged woman staring back at me!* Frankly, I don't like what I see: the lip lines, the crow's feet, the turkey waddle, the bat wings. I have tried to halt the aging process, but it's coming at me like a freight train, and there's no stopping it. My arsenal of beauty products promise younger-looking skin, but no amount of face cream or retinol will make me look thirty again. Why is it so hard to love our bodies? We can do nothing to stop the aging process. It's inevitable. But we can work on refining our inner beauty. Our outward beauty may fade as we get older, but our inner beauty is being refined like precious gold. The older we get, the wiser we become, as each new experience helps us develop a more beautiful spirit.

I used to work with a plastic surgeon, and he remarked that patients return to him over and over again for more surgery because they are never pleased with their bodies. Until those women heal their self-image, they will never be happy with themselves, no matter how much surgery they have. Most of the surgeries I assisted were breast enhancements, but one day

I assisted a total body lift which was an eight-hour surgery. That woman's body had an incision almost the entire circumference of her midsection. I can't imagine the pain she experienced upon waking up from this horrendous surgery. I don't understand how someone can put themselves at risk for blood clots, stroke, and adhesions—all for the sake of vanity.

Our worth is not determined by our outward appearance. Unfortunately, society strongly influences body dysmorphic disorder. We see perfect photos on social media that have been photoshopped and filtered. It's no wonder we are constantly examining ourselves to see if we measure up. I heard about a study that showed when people "detox" from social media, it lowers feelings of depression because they stop comparing themselves to posts of perfect pictures. Sometimes a smile is all it takes to be beautiful. A joyful heart enhances everyone's beauty.

The aging process is just another part of our journey through life, whether we like it or not. As your outer appearance begins to fade, remember that

the fountain of youth lies within your heart and becomes more beautiful with time. We may lose the elasticity in our skin and the luster in our eyes, and our bodies may become weak and feeble, but our hearts can flourish with the unfading beauty of God's grace. It's just a part of our journey. Every day is a gift from God, and because of His grace, we can embrace our journey, knowing that outward wasting away means inwardly we are being renewed. Embrace yourself!

Your beauty should not come from outward adornment, such as elaborate hairstyles, and wearing of gold jewelry or clothes. Rather, it should be that of your inner self, the unfading beauty of a gentle and quiet spirit, which is of great worth in the sight of God.

1 PETER 3:3-4

33
The Joy of Little Boys

So I say to you: Ask and it will be given to you; seek, and you will find; knock and the door will be opened to you. For everyone who asks, receives; the one who seeks finds; and to the one who knocks, the door will be opened. LUKE 11:9–10

THE BOYS IN OUR FAMILY love to test the limits at an early age. They carefully plan a scheme or tactic to help them manipulate and irritate anyone who crosses their path. When my grandson Joshua was two years old, he wanted his mother, Elizabeth, to know that he was in charge. He watched her go out the back door, then he swiftly locked the deadbolt. He looked her in the eye through the glass patio door and demanded, "Like it?" Luckily, Elizabeth had the key in her pocket and was able to let herself back in. Years later, history repeated itself when my grandson, Jeremiah, did the same thing at the wonderful age of two, only his reaction was quite different. He peered through the glass at his mother trying to open the door. When he realized what he had done, he burst into tears, throwing himself onto the floor. As Elizabeth helplessly watched Jeremiah thrashing on the floor, his big sisters, Sierra and Kaylee, ran around the house and got in through the unlocked front door.

You would think that after hearing both of these stories, a grandmother would have enough sense not to ever leave a toddler alone in the house, even for a brief moment. Well, I was babysitting my two grandsons, six-year-old Jacob and Justin who was three, when I realized I had left one of their jackets in my car and needed to go back out and get it. Since Jacob was busy watching his favorite show, and Justin was quietly sitting on the couch with his tablet, I thought it would be a good time to sneak out without either of them noticing. *Besides*, I thought to myself, *I know the garage code and I have a garage remote in my car*. I hurried out to the car, hoping the boys wouldn't see me slip out the door. I pulled the jacket out of my car, and when I turned around, Jacob was standing behind me. He asked, "Where are you going?" I quickly reassured him, "I'm just getting your jacket; I'm not going anywhere." My heart picked up speed as I nervously trotted back to the front door, and low and behold, it was locked! A chill ran down my spine. Justin peered at us through the sidelight with a huge smile on his face. I pleaded, "Justin, unlock the door." He tried but was unable to do it. I ran to the keypad by the garage and punched in the code but nothing happened. My panic escalated as I hurried to my car and opened the center console to get the garage remote. It wasn't there! I had left it in my other car. I prayed in desperation, "Dear God, please help us get back into the house!" We returned to the front door, and tried to coax Justin to unlock the door. He kept trying but was unable to do it. By now Jacob was getting worried too. He made hand gestures, trying to show his little brother how to unlock the door, but it was useless. I thought to myself, *If only I had followed my instincts to grab my phone before going outside, I would be able to call my son or daughter-in-law to get the new garage code.* As I stood on the porch, helplessly peering through the sidelight at my precious grandson who was totally unaware of the danger he was in, my mind kept chanting, *John and Julie are never going to let me babysit again!*

My thoughts were interrupted when I realized I could make a call from my watch, if I was close enough to my phone inside the house. It worked!! I called Julie, but her phone was on silent because she was at a rehearsal. My son, John, was away on business in another state. I knew I had to swallow my pride and call him, but I worried he might be in a meeting and unable to take my call. I dialed the number and held my breath as I said a silent prayer, "Please God, let him answer!" Praise the Lord, he answered! I blurted out, "John, I'm locked out of your house and Justin is inside by himself. What is the garage code so I can get back in?" In a very calm, unalarming, tone he gave me the code but said he has been having trouble getting the pad to work. I ran to the garage and punched in the code. It didn't work, and I lost his call. Almost in tears and on the verge of panic, I went back to the door and miraculously, the knob turned and we were able to get back inside. Justin was quietly sitting on the couch, sheepishly grinning at me as if nothing had happened. John, who had remained calm and level-headed, must have trusted me to handle the situation because his only comment was, "I was disappointed, because I wanted to use my new smart garage opener to open it from Dallas." To this day, we don't know how the door got unlocked. Once I got inside and calmed down, I locked the door and asked Justin to unlock it for me . . . but he couldn't do it. I believe God had heard my prayers, came to my rescue, and opened the door for us. I will never understand why boys need to be in charge, take risks, and test the limits! Thank you, Lord, for coming to my rescue.

*Do not be anxious about anything,
but in every situation, by prayer and petition,
with thanksgiving, present your requests to God.*

PHILIPPIANS 4:6

34
Be Still

*Very early in the morning, while it was still dark,
Jesus got up, left the house and went off to a
solitary place, where he prayed.*

MARK 1:35

I REMEMBER THE DAYS when I had four children at home constantly demanding my attention. I had no time for myself except for the blissful, brief moments of silence when they took their naps or went to a friend's house. Even when they were too old for a nap but not quite a teenager, I established a quiet time when they had to go to their rooms to read a book or play quietly. I would use that time to read or write in my journal or sew, and I cherished those few moments to recharge myself.

I have learned, to truly relax and experience peace, I need to get away from the messy house, the dirty dishes, and the endless laundry. As I write this, my nest is quiet and empty; however, I still have dirty dishes, piles of laundry (though a bit smaller), and weeds poking their heads up from my garden. My husband and I still like to get away from all the responsibilities and chores around the house to forget about all the daily stressors of life. We live in Illinois where the terrain is mostly flat, but we discovered a place not too far away that makes us feel like we have escaped to the mountains. The Shawnee National Forest is near the southern border of

Illinois, lying between the Mississippi and Ohio Rivers. It is known for the dramatic rock formation called Camel Rock, which stands tall overlooking the forest canopy below. The panoramic views are spectacular, and even though it may not be a mountain, it sure feels like one when standing on the rock jutting out over the bluff.

When I was there, I felt so small on top of that enormous rock, like I was merely a shadow in comparison to God. As I stood in the silence overlooking the lush green forest below, it gave me instant peace, and my instinct was to *be still* as I felt the presence of God.

Jesus quite often would find solitude on a mountain, away from people and the daily demands, so He could be alone to pray.

"But Jesus Himself would often slip away to the wilderness and pray" (Luke 5:16 NASB).

"And after He had sent the crowds away, He went up on the mountain by Himself to pray. and when it was evening, He was there alone." (Matthew 14:23 NASB)

When Moses wrote the Ten Commandments, he was on a mountain. The transfiguration of Christ was on a high mountain, and Jesus prayed on the Mount of Olives the night before His crucifixion. It is no wonder I feel closer to God when I'm in the mountains. When I find time to be still, to reflect on who He is and all He has done for me, and all He is going to do in my future, I am in awe. Find your peaceful place—and listen.

Be still, and know that I am God; I will be exalted among the nations, I will be exalted in the earth.

PSALM 46:10

35
A New Day

*Let the morning bring me word of your unfailing love,
for I have put my trust in you. Show me the way
I should go, for to you I entrust my life.*

PSALM 143:8

WHEN I WOKE UP on the morning of my fortieth birthday, I was very depressed at the thought of entering the next decade of life. I didn't want to get out of bed, so I just lay there under the warm, cozy blankets. My husband came into the bedroom and placed a freshly brewed cup of coffee on the nightstand, then crawled into bed with me and chirped, "Happy Birthday!" I was not amused by the smirk on his face. I asked, "Why aren't you ready for work?" He mused, "Because I'm not going to work today. I took the day off to spend it with you!" I perked right up, and suddenly, the day didn't seem so gloomy anymore. I sat up in bed and took a sip of my coffee. "What should we do today? Did you make any plans?" He gave me a quick kiss and smiled. "Come downstairs. I have a surprise for you."

The adrenaline rushed through my veins as I jumped out of bed. I wondered what it might be: Had he bought doughnuts? Or maybe a new comfy chair? Or could it be a new car? (I knew it wasn't a car, but ten years later, for my fiftieth birthday, he bought me a Z28 Camaro.) I headed toward the kitchen and was greeted with a beautiful, fresh bouquet of flowers and a chic wicker picnic basket. I opened the clasp and raised the lid. It was filled with snacks, green grapes, a bottle of sparkling grape juice, two champagne flutes, and a sweet birthday card. He took me in his arms and I gazed into his sultry brown eyes as he divulged, "I thought we would go on a picnic for lunch, and maybe take a walk along the riverfront." I melted into his arms, overwhelmed with love, admiration, and devotion for the man who had perfected the art of pulling my heartstrings.

When I woke up that morning, with a dark cloud hovering over my head, I had no idea it would turn out to become such a great memory. Mike had turned my sad day into something really fun. He knew I loved surprises.

God and Jesus were the masters of surprises. For starters, Jesus was born to a virgin mother that He created! He caused a lame man to leap and a mute man to speak. He calmed a raging storm, walked on water, brought a child back to life, gave sight to the blind and turned water into wine. God spoke from a burning bush, made a donkey speak and sent angels to shepherds announcing His Son's birth. The biggest surprise was Christ's resurrection. Even though He had repeatedly told His followers it would happen, they were still surprised when He rose from the dead and appeared to them. God will never cease to amaze us with his power and grace. I think He enjoys surprising us, as much as we enjoy being surprised.

The steadfast love of the LORD never ceases; his mercies never come to an end they are new every morning; great is your faithfulness.

LAMENTATIONS 3:22-23 ESV

36

The Storms Will Come

Pray without ceasing.
1 THESSALONIANS 5:17 ESV

𝓘 **COULD HEAR THE RUMBLE** of thunder in the distance as we prepared for the severe storm headed in our direction. The weather channel warned it could bring hail, high winds, and power outages. I put the patio chair cushions in the storage trunk, lowered the patio umbrella, and made sure all the windows in the house were shut. I went to the basement to roll up the area rugs and placed them on top of an old couch in case the basement flooded. Back upstairs, I curled up in my overstuffed chair and got lost in a good book to forget about the impending rain. About halfway through chapter 2, the storm raged outside as predicted, and the lights went out. I worried the basement would flood because, without power, the sump pump would not be able to remove water from the foundation of our newly built home. Every house we've ever owned has had a flooded basement, so it was a very legitimate concern. Mike grabbed a chair and a flashlight, and prepared to bail water. He couldn't quite see the water level in the sump pit, so he adjusted the cover to keep an eye on it as it began to rise.

After three long hours of keeping vigil, finally, the power came back on, but Mike was not prepared for what happened next. When he had adjusted the cover, he inadvertently disconnected the pipe, and as soon as the power resumed, a geyser of filthy groundwater suddenly shot up to the ceiling, flooding that corner of the basement. He quickly lunged forward into the fountain of muddy water and pulled the plug, cutting off power to the pump—it's a wonder he didn't get electrocuted. As he stood there, with water dripping down his face, I couldn't help but laugh! He made the necessary adjustments before plugging it back in, and the pump started doing its job again.

We were fortunate that particular storm was of no consequence, but sometimes the storms of life can wreak havoc on our lives. One day, everything is tidy in its place, then a tornado blows through, turning order into chaos, and life becomes a nightmare. It catches us off guard, and we stand there shell-shocked, trying to make sense of it all. The good news is—storms don't last forever. But how do we prepare for those afflictions?

When a storm is brewing, we need to make sure we have Jesus in the boat. We must first have a relationship with Christ, followed by studying

His Word, communing with Him in prayer, and memorizing Scripture. We need to be ready. When we get out of fellowship, we aren't as inclined to turn to God for help as a first response. Our instinct will be to take control of the situation ourselves rather than turning to God, which leaves us feeling helpless. Christ warned us there would be trials in this life, but He also promised to help us through those hard times. Storms can be necessary, because it's during those times that the roots go deeper to hang on for dear life; the toughest times are actually when we do most of our growing. Sometimes He sends thunder to get our attention forcing us to rely on Him. Have faith that He will carry you through the storms, because He will.

I have told you these things, so that in me you may have peace. In this world you will have trouble. But take heart! I have overcome the world.

JOHN 16:33

37
I Hereby Banish You Forever

*I praise you because I am fearfully and wonderfully made;
your works are wonderful, I know that full well.*

PSALM 139:14

I CAN REMEMBER as early as third grade being called names because of my red hair. The taunts continued through high school from cruel kids who seemed to be born without a conscience. Those ugly names damaged my self-image, and for a long time I felt self-conscious and inferior. I was called names like carrot top, rusted brain, Irish setter, and Bozo, among others that I can't mention here. Probably the most painful chant I ever heard was "I'd rather be dead than red in the head"; it made me feel like I was the ugliest kid on earth.

It was humiliating to be criticized for the color of my hair. I felt like a freak and wanted to hide. It took many years before I was able to love and accept myself because, for a long time, I believed those insults my classmates hurled at me. Yet, I am a stronger person today because I had to learn how to overcome those negative comments. All those bullies had mean spirits, but as I listened to their taunts, I grew tougher skin as I learned how to let it roll off my shoulders and walk away from them. I always held my tongue because retaliating is not what God would want me to do.

After years of self-talk and reassurance, I learned to love myself and embrace my red hair. I decided to banish those hurtful words from my childhood forever because I needed to believe I was worth more than that. It seems silly to let classmates affect my self-worth, but the insults bombarding me had damaged my dignity, and it wasn't easy to repair the wounds that had marred my self-image. I had to erase those negative feelings by making a decree: *I hereby banish you forever!*

There is a story in Luke 13:10–17 where Jesus is teaching in a synagogue on the Sabbath and He notices a woman bent over and crippled. He beckoned her over to Himself and touched her, healing her, and she was able to straighten upright after nearly two decades of being hunched over. The spectators immediately harassed Him for healing on the Sabbath, but Jesus rebuked them saying, "You hypocrites! Doesn't each of you on the Sabbath untie his ox or donkey from the stall and lead it out to give it water? Then should not this woman, a daughter of Abraham, whom Satan has kept bound for eighteen long years, be set free on the Sabbath day from what bound her?" (vv. 15–16).

Jesus had spotted that woman among the crowd and had compassion on her. When you believe the lies and insults you've heard for years, it's hard to believe anything else. It can make you feel alone amid a crowded auditorium and you may wonder, *where is God*? He wants you to know that He sees you, just like the bent over woman who was probably invisible to the crowd, but not to Jesus. He sees the pain and suffering from abuse, but His love can heal those wounds.

He heals the brokenhearted and binds up their wounds.

PSALM 147:3

38

It's Never Too Late

I can do all things through him who strengthens me.

PHILIPPIANS 4:13 ESV

I DIDN'T GO TO COLLEGE IMMEDIATELY following high school because, after twelve years of school, I couldn't wait to graduate and never have to study again. My biggest ambition in life was to be a stay-at-home mom, so when I had my first child at age twenty, my husband granted my wish and told me I could quit my job to care for our precious baby girl, Elizabeth. Fourteen months later, our son, John was born, and I was the happiest mom ever. I loved being home with my children. When they were ten and eleven years old, I become a foster parent because I loved being a mother so much I wanted to share my passion with those less fortunate. We ended up adopting two babies, Abigail and Hannah. I had to stop taking in foster babies because I knew that if I didn't, we would end up with ten kids.

As I entered my mid-thirties, the busiest time in my life, something changed inside me. I realized I had a great responsibility to raise those four beautiful children, but I feared if something were to happen to my husband, I wouldn't be able to financially support them. Mike encouraged me to take one college course to see if I could do it and to give me the confidence to pursue my aspirations. To my surprise, I got an A, which was a total shock since I never applied myself in high school and got terrible grades. I was surprised that I actually loved learning. College wasn't anything like high school. I had a completely different attitude toward school, knowing my degree would help me provide for my family.

So, after anatomy and physiology, I took microbiology and got the highest grade in the class. I was ecstatic, and it gave me the burning desire to pursue my dream of becoming a registered nurse. While my very patient husband cared for two very demanding toddlers and two adolescents in the midst of searching for their identities, I was able to complete my degree. If it weren't for him, I would not have been able to do it. I never thought I could achieve something so rewarding. I'm glad I conquered my fears and decided to get a college education, despite my very busy life.

It's never too late to change your life, to set a new course, and to pursue your dreams. I've been a nurse for twenty-plus years, and it has been very rewarding. I have had multiple opportunities to share Christ with dying patients, and have had the joy of showing God's love to many hurting people. I realized it was God's purpose for me to become a nurse. I became a wife and mother first and foremost, then a nurse. God can use anyone for His glory if they are willing. It's never too late to seek His will for your life and change your course. God has a plan for you, and He will make a way for you to fulfill it.

*Commit to the Lord whatever you do,
and he will establish your plans.*

PROVERBS 16:3

39
God Is Writing Your Story

The heart of man plans his way,
but the Lord establishes his steps.
PROVERBS 16:9 ESV

We all love a good story—we love reading them, hearing them, and watching them being played out on the movie screen. The more conflict to keep us on the edge of our seat, the better; otherwise, it would be boring. Even though we love reading and watching stories of loss and tragedy, we don't want any of it in our lives, yet somehow it always manages to weave itself in when we least expect it.

Whatever you are going through right now, no matter how painful it may be, it is not beyond the providence of God. You can trust Him to be the author of your story and to rescue you whenever your life goes from drama to horror. He is our heavenly Father who watches out for His children. When your children cry out for help because they are scared or hurt, the minute you hear their pleas, you run. You don't walk, you run to them, because you sense the urgency, and all you want to do is stop their pain and fear. You want to hold them in your arms, embrace them, and comfort them until they don't hurt anymore. That is how God responds to us when we cry out for help.

Suffering changes us. Sometimes, God uses it to draw us closer to Him. The trials we face help to mold us into the person God wants us to be. Everything we overcome, with God's strength, prepares us to face what is ahead. We can trust God's hand to continue writing our story, which will end with His sovereign purpose. We may be confused by the heartache, drama, and villains that pop into our lives, but when we get to the last chapter, we will be in awe and wonder of the work He has done and how He used each painful struggle to get us to the end of our story.

When I adopted two babies born to drug-addicted mothers, I thought I knew how their stories would pan out. I would rescue them from possible abandonment, hunger, neglect, abuse, and being exposed to a life of drug addiction and destruction. I thought that by teaching them about God and how to live according to His laws, they would choose to put Him first in their lives. But there was an unexpected plot twist, and one of them got into trouble with the law just after high school. She spent time in prison because she was in the company of someone who committed a crime. She has been homeless and has lived at the Salvation Army shelter. She has experimented with drugs and alcohol to numb her painful decisions. She went on a roller-coaster ride of returning to God, then abandoning Him multiple times. I felt

like a failure and blamed myself for her destructive behavior, but I learned to accept the fact that she had a sinful nature and was making her own choices. I also realized this could have easily happened to my biological children but, thankfully, it didn't. I have to trust God to finish writing her story because I know He has great plans for her life. The best thing I can do is pray for her and let her know that I love her unconditionally, no matter what. That will never change, and she knows it. I have peace knowing that all four of my children have made a confession of faith and know the Lord as their Savior. I have joy knowing two of my children are training up their children in Christian homes and both of them are leading Bible studies. That gives me so much joy. I don't take any credit for that; it is the Holy Spirit working in them. I realize I am not the one writing my daughter's story, nor have I ever been, but I can trust God to finish it, and in His time He will.

For now we see in a mirror dimly, but then face to face.
Now I know in part, then I shall know fully,
even as I have been fully known.

1 CORINTHIANS 13:12 ESV

40
Our Days Are Numbered

*Teach us to number our days, that we
may gain a heart of wisdom.*

PSALM 90:12

AS TIME MOVES ON, and the aging process takes its toll, I feel like I'm racing downhill and the brakes aren't working so I keep picking up speed and momentum. I know my end is closer than my beginning, and I have so many things that I still want to accomplish—so many places to see, and so many people to love as much as possible. I don't want to miss a beat! People say, when our lives are over, we won't be remembered by what we've done, how much money we've made, or how many treasures we've accumulated, but they will remember how we made them feel. When I'm old and gray, I want to look back knowing my life reflected God's love.

When Christ came to earth, He was ordained to die in our place. His purpose was to save us by taking the punishment for our sins so we could live with Him in eternity. His days were numbered, and His time on earth was spent preparing the world for His death.

One of our primary goals in life is to prepare for our departure. It may seem like a morbid thought, and while most people don't like to think about death, we should focus on how to live out our days. Don't let your life be like a boat drifting out to sea. Stand at the helm and have a destination in mind and pursue it. Follow your path, fulfill a dream, build a legacy for the next generation to emulate. You have been given another day to be better than yesterday, to touch a life, to experience joy, to seek God's will, and to be more than you thought you could be. If you have a pulse, you still have a purpose.

Don't wait for New Year's Day to make resolutions. Why not make every day a new beginning to be transformed into something beautiful? I have heard so many times, *If I can do it, anyone can!* We have choices to make every hour of every day. Every choice we make sets in motion the outcome of tomorrow. And not just for us; our decisions have the potential to not only change us, but the ripple effect can also influence somebody else. Life is precious and each day is a gift, so spend it wisely, and don't take it for granted.

I see my life as an opportunity to accomplish God's Will. I don't think of it in terms of how many days I have left because I don't know the answer to that. I speculate that I could have forty more years ahead of me if I live to be a centenarian. It's exciting to think I might still have many years left to fulfill my purpose, to tell others about Christ, and to be the best wife, mother, and grandmother I can be!

Our days are numbered. Life is precious. May you seek Christ in all the things that give you joy and peace as you find the *grace to embrace* your journey through life.

> *You saw me before I was born. Every day of my life was recorded in your book. Every moment was laid out before a single day had passed*
>
> PSALM 139:16 NLT

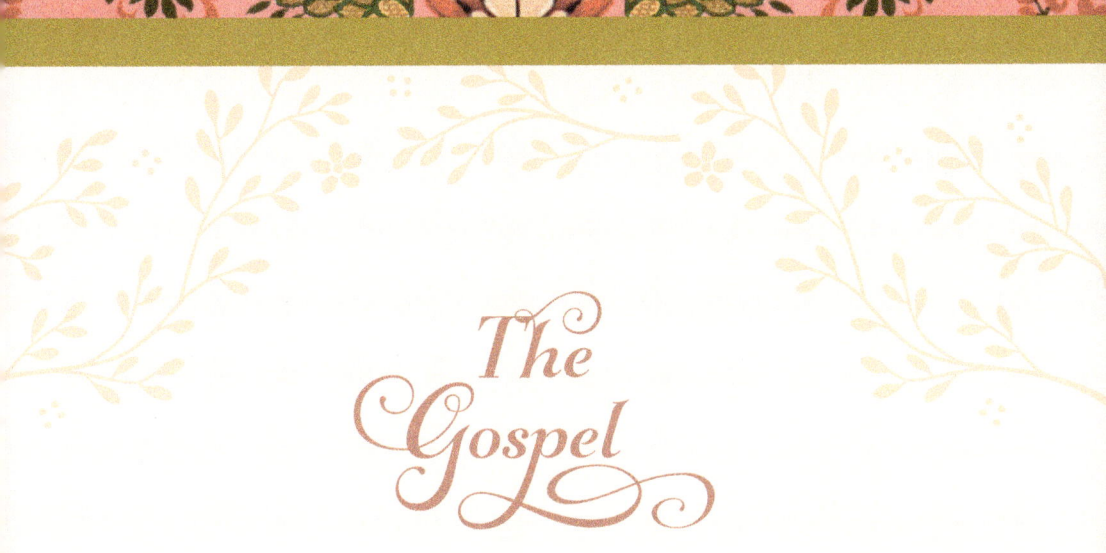

The Gospel

IN THESE DAYS OF UNCERTAINTY, we all could use some good news, and here it is: God loves you and has a plan for your life. Are you broken and you don't know what to do? Are you searching for something more to this life but don't know where to find it?

Jesus can rescue you. He is the only one who can fill the emptiness in your heart. The Bible says, in spite of our wickedness, God loves us. He is waiting to receive you with open arms and forgive all your sins. He loves you so much that He sent His only Son to die in your place. Jesus is the only door into heaven.

THE PROBLEM: We all have sinned.

> *"For all have sinned and fall short of the glory of God."*
> ROMANS 3:23 ESV

> *"For the wages of sin is death,*
> *but the free gift of God is eternal life in Christ Jesus our Lord."*
> ROMANS 6:23 ESV

THE SOLUTION: Jesus

> *"For God so loved the world, that he gave his only Son,*
> *that whoever believes in him should not perish but have eternal life."*
> JOHN 3:16 ESV

> *"If you confess with your mouth that Jesus is Lord and believe*
> *in your heart that God raised him from the dead, you will be saved.*
> *For with the heart one believes and is justified,*
> *and with the mouth one confesses and is saved."*
> ROMANS 10:9–10 ESV

If you are ready to become a child of God and enter into His family, you can pray something like this:

Dear heavenly Father, I know that I'm a sinner, and I ask for your forgiveness. I believe Jesus died on the cross to pay the penalty for my sins and rose from the dead. I trust you as my Lord and Savior and ask that you come into my life. In Jesus name, amen!

If you prayed that prayer, congratulations, and welcome to the family of God! I would encourage you to read the Bible (God's Word to us) so you can learn about God's principles and how you should live as a believer and so you can develop a close relationship with your heavenly Father. Find a Bible-teaching church so you can grow, learn, and have fellowship with other believers, and get baptized, which is the next step, as you commit your life to serving God.

Author's Note

Dear Reader,

When I had the idea to write this book, I have to admit that I had no idea how difficult writing would be. There were so many days I pleaded with God, "If you want me to write this, I need your help because I can't do it on my own!" I felt so inadequate and out of my realm, but I knew if it was God's Will, I needed to be obedient. I will be the first to admit, *I am not worthy to write this book*. Sometimes God asks us to do things we don't feel capable of doing so we follow through out of love and obedience. With God as my guide, these stories were written from my heart to yours.

This book contains forty stories in honor of my fortieth anniversary. The Bible has many stories that contain the number forty as a time of testing and preparing for something good with the common theme: *Don't give up!* Marriage takes a lot of love, forgiveness, and devotion, but God has been faithful and has shown me the grace I need to embrace my journey. I look forward to the years ahead. If forty is a time of preparation, something good must be around the corner.

My prayer is for this book to encourage anyone going through similar circumstances, to remind you that you are not alone, and to inspire you to write about your own journey. If my stories help only one person, then it will be worth more than I could have ever asked.

Acknowledgments

WRITING THIS BOOK was much like giving birth; but it was a labor of love written for all who will read it. When I began this journey, I had great anticipation and excitement, but it wasn't long before the painful process got intense and the anguish slowed me down, even causing me to stop at times, as if in false labor. Many times I wanted to quit. But thankfully, my journey continued with perseverance and determination, and finally—I am happy to announce—I have birthed my first book, and it's exhilarating!

In my home office, the following verse has been displayed on my whiteboard, motivating me to keep racing toward the finish line and to persevere until the book is completed:

> *So do not throw away your confidence; it will be richly rewarded. You need to persevere so that when you have done the will of God, you will receive what he has promised.* HEBREWS 10:35-36

I FIRST WANT TO THANK THE LORD for prompting me to write and never giving up on me. There were so many days when I'd tell Him, "I can't do this!" but He gave me the strength and affirmation I needed to carry on.

But He said to me, "My grace is sufficient for you, for my power is made perfect in weakness. Therefore, I will boast all the more gladly about my weaknesses, so that Christ's power may rest on me. That is why, for Christ's sake, I delight in weaknesses, in insults, in hardships, in persecutions, in difficulties. For when I am weak, then I am strong." 2 CORINTHIANS 12:9–10

TO MY HUSBAND, MIKE: Words cannot express my gratitude for the blessing you are to me. Thank you for your unconditional love, for believing in me and supporting me through this endeavor and bringing me a cup of Earl Grey tea when I was hard at work. You endured listening to all my thoughts and ideas without walking away in exasperation. I also want to thank you for illustrating the children's book we did together for our grandchildren in 2017. You've brought life to so many of my dreams, including this book, and for that I am eternally grateful. I love you with all my heart.

THANKS TO MY CHILDREN, Elizabeth, John, Abigail, and Hannah, for your love and support in everything I do. You are such an encouragement to me, and I am blessed to be your mother. You all have filled my life with love and adventure. Thanks for letting me write about it—I love you.

A special thanks to my daughter, Elizabeth Hitz, for taking time out of her very busy life to read my work and give me the affirmation I needed to keep going. That means so much to me—thank you.

TO ALL OF MY BEAUTIFUL GRANDCHILDREN: Joan Christine, Mariah, Joshua, Sierra, Kaylee, Jacob, Justin, Josiah, Jeremiah, Jax, and all the rest yet to be born: I love you from the bottom of my heart, and I'm so thankful for the blessing you are to me. I pray you will seek God's direction in everything you do while you create your own beautiful memories. You give me more joy than you will ever know. You are the sunshine on my darkest days.

TO MY FATHER, WALTER DUNCAN LOTT: I am so blessed and thankful to have been raised in a Christian home where God was the center of our lives. You have passed down the legacy of your father, Walter E. Lott, who was instrumental in starting our home church and teaching so many people with his knowledge and wisdom. I am impressed by your devotion to faithfully continue teaching God's Word to your Sunday school class at the age of eighty-three. Thanks, Dad, for taking me to church every week—and for dragging me out the door a few times when I was in junior high and didn't want to go to evening church. You instilled in me the importance of faith and values, which are being passed down to my children and theirs. What a great legacy. I love you.

TO MY LATE MOTHER: I wish you were here so I could tell you that I am so grateful for the unconditional love you gave me. Thank you for inspiring me with your love, patience, and servant heart that helped shape me into the person I am today. You were an amazing mom, and I am forever grateful. I love you so much and look forward to the day I will see you again.

THANK YOU TO MY SWEET SISTERS, Deborah Compton and Jennifer Anglin, and my brother, Ted Lott, and their spouses. I am so blessed to have you by my side through everything. We have shared so many great memories, and I look forward to many more.

I ALSO WANT TO THANK MY EXTENDED FAMILY. You all have taught me what it means to embrace family gatherings and to support each other through trials and losses as well as joyous celebrations. You are the foundation of love that will be passed down through the generations. What a blessing.

Finally, I want to give a very special thanks to my UNCLE TED REED for being such a great inspiration to me. Your positive attitude and generous spirit have touched my heart. Whenever you have struggled with health issues or inclement weather, making it difficult for you to care for your "dependents" (as you referred to your horses), you always rose above your circumstances and maintained a happy disposition. If I can be half as positive and active as you at the age of eighty-six, I will be so blessed!

IMAGE CREDITS

Cover and interior illustration old baroque tapestry © by Nicoolay/istock.com by Gettyimages. All rights reserved.

Cover and interior image pink peonies copyright © by Vetre/Shutterstock.com. All rights reserved.

All photographs are property of their respective copyright holders, and all rights are reserved.

Images Chatper 1: Dahlia, pages 28, 50, 58, 68, 90, 92, 94, 96, 115, 118, 120, 122, 126, 142, by the author.

Chapter 1: Beautiful pink flowers by Mary Betcher, Unsplash.com.

Chapter 2: Warbler by Noah Sillyman, Unsplash.com/Butterfly by Bob Brewer, Unsplash.com.

Chapter 3: Pink clouds by Kenrick Mills, Unsplash.com/Eagle by Patrick Hendrey, Unsplash.com.

Chapter 4: Linn Cove viaduct, Linville US by Wes Hicks, Unsplash.com/Rhythm of the mountains by Sergey Pesterev, Unsplash.com.

Chapter 5: Promenade by Zibik, Unsplash.com.

Chapter 6: Sunset field by Sapan Patel/Baby's hand by Elizabeth Hitz Photography

Chapter 7: Ruehampton University, London, UK by Carlita Benazito/Showa. Kinen Park by Norikio Yamamoto, Unsplash.com

Chapter 8: Christmas tree candles by Annie Spratt, Unsplash.com.

Chapter 9: Palmyra Cove Nature Park, Palmyra US by Ray Hennessey, Unsplash.com.

Chapter 10: Wedding dinner table flower by Lanty/Bride and groom holding hands by Wu Jianxiong, Unsplash.com.

Chapter 11: Grapes by Dan-Cristian Paduret, Unsplash.com/Hydrangeas by David Cooper, unsplash.com.

Chapter 12: Avalon, NJ, US by Barth Bailey, Unsplash.com.

Chapter 13: Chubby buddy by Clever Visuals, Unsplash.com.

Chapter 14: Baby feet by Gigin Krishnan, Unsplash.com.

Chapter 15: Thankful napkin ring by Debbie Hudson, Unsplash.com.

Chapter 16: Toledo Botanical Garden, Toledo, OH by Gary Bendig, Unsplash.com.

Chapter 17: Springtime by Bill Fairs, Unsplash.com

Chapter 18: Mother bird protecting her young by Ray Hennessey, Unsplash.com.

Chapter 19: Bible and a cup of tea by Carolyn V, Unsplash.com.

Chapter 20: Fresh lavender buds by Sharon McCutcheon, Unsplash.com.

Chapter 21: Days like this by OC Ganzalez, Unsplash.com/Bleeding Heart by Yoksel Zok, Unsplash.com.

Chapter 22: Cattle Dog by Patrick Hendry, Unsplash.com.

Chapter 25: Pink Gerbera up close by Andrew Small, Unsplash.com.

Chapter 26: Pig by Christopher Carson, Unsplash.com./Pig on the move by Annie Spratt, Unsplash.com.

Chapter 27: Soft comforts by Alexander Possingham, Unsplash.com.

Chapter 28: Lantern by William Luiz, Unsplash.com.

Chapter 29: Cutest little ducks by Jennie Bess, Unsplash.com.

Chapter 33: Grey pigeon by Sneha, Unsplash.com.

Chapter 34: Serra da Estrela, Portugal by Louis Estima, Unsplash.com

Chapter 35: Picnic by Katie Hliznitsova, Unsplash.com.

Chapter 37: Redhead Journey continues by Colton Sturgeon. Unsplash.com.

Chapter 38: Fall leaves, Minnesota Landscape Arboretum, Chaska, MN by Shannon Kunkle, Unsplash.com.

Chapter 39: Pink-toned thoughts on a hike by Simon Berger, Unsplash.com.

Chapter 40 Lake Atitilán, Guatemala by Mark Harpur, Unsplash.com.

www.ingramcontent.com/pod-product-compliance
Lightning Source LLC
Chambersburg PA
CBHW040638100526
44583CB00037B/3046